D1237268

# POLITICAL LEADERSHIP IN A SOUTHERN CITY

## New Orleans in the Progressive Era, 1896-1902

The McGinty Monograph Series


Billy H. Gilley, Editor


Published Titles:

ISRAEL SHREVE: REVOLUTIONARY WAR OFFICER
By William Y. Thompson

DENIS-NICOLAS FOUCAULT AND THE
NEW ORLEANS REBELLION OF 1768
By Carl A. Brasseaux

POLITICAL LEADERSHIP IN A SOUTHERN CITY
NEW ORLEANS IN THE PROGRESSIVE ERA, 1896-1902
By Edward F. Haas

# POLITICAL LEADERSHIP IN A SOUTHERN CITY

New Orleans in the Progressive Era,
1896-1902

By Edward F. Haas

McGINTY

PUBLICATIONS

DEPARTMENT OF HISTORY
LOUISIANA TECH UNIVERSITY

Ruston, Louisiana

1988

Printed in the United States of America

Library of Congress Catalog Number: 88-60326
ISBN 0-940231-04-2

*To Karen*

# CONTENTS

# ILLUSTRATIONS

These photographs and sketches will be found following page 59:

# FOREWORD

Urban political machines have rarely characterized the South. One exception was turn-of-the-century New Orleans. In *Political Leadership in a Southern City: New Orleans in the Progressive Era, 1896-1902*, Edward F. Haas describes how rapid population growth and ethnic diversity based on the influx of immigrants and blacks, the drive to preserve white supremacy, and Democratic Party control (the latter two carryovers from Reconstruction) facilitated machine domination. Other ingredients were violence based on nativism and racism, economic debt, and government corruption.

By virtue of its focus on New Orleans politics and its detailed analysis of the ethnic makeup, political and business orientation, and ward residence of the political leaders, the book chronicles an important aspect of Louisiana history.

In the struggle for power, Haas describes how Regular Democrats catered to working class whites and immigrants and controlled them through tight-knit ward and precinct organization in order to dominate the more reform-minded business and professional Citizens' Leaguers. Although bitter rivals, the two Democratic factions combined to dominate Louisiana politics until the advent of Huey Long in 1928.

Billy H. Gilley

# ACKNOWLEDGEMENTS

Writing a book is perhaps the loneliest cooperative venture known to mankind. In the final analysis, a book is the product of an individual's personal and often private communion with a topic. One knowing observer has contended that this communion commonly takes the form of staring at one's writing implement—in my case, first a pad and pencil, later a typewriter and finally a computer keyboard—until beads of blood appear on the writer's forehead. Although I have not physically bled, I must confess to a more realistic understanding of the term sanguine.

Historians incur a battery of debts before they reach that critical level of thoughtful bleeding. I am no different. Librarians and archivists have assisted me throughout this project. Rose Lambert, Louisiana Historical Center, Louisiana State Museum, supplied me with an unending wealth of sources that usually included information that no one else could find. Collin B. Hamer, Wayne M. Everard and Jean Jones, Louisiana Division, New Orleans Public Library; Jane Stevens and Gay Craft, Louisiana Collection, Howard-Tilton Memorial Library, Tulane University; and Wilbur E. Meneray, Department of Manuscripts and Archives, Tulane University, were equally eager to help.

Glen Jeansonne, University of Wisconsin, Milwaukee; Stephen Webre, Louisiana Tech University; and Steven G. Reinhardt, Louisiana Endowment for the Humanities, encouraged me to turn several related essays into a book; they read all or parts of the manuscript, made valuable suggestions for improvements and sustained me with their friendship. G. Rollie Adams, Director of the Louisiana State Museum, has created a pleasant working environment and always extended his support for my endeavors. Louis R. Harlan and John Duffy, University of Maryland, College Park, have been outstanding mentors as well as firm friends. So, too, has been Bennett H. Wall, University of Georgia. Glenn R. Conrad, managing editor of *Louisiana History*, kindly granted permission to reprint material that had previously appeared in that publication. A research grant from the American Association for State and Local History assisted with the research for Chapter 4. B. H. Gilley, Louisiana Tech University, head of the McGinty Publications, guided the manuscript through the pitfalls of publication. His concern for excellence and his friendship were evident at all times during the production of this volume. I, nevertheless, must claim full responsibility for any errors that may appear in these pages.

Special appreciation must go to my wife Karen. She endured many nights when her husband was clenched in mortal combat with his computer and numerous days when his mind belonged wholly to a group of long dead politicians. She, nonetheless, was always loving and supportive, often raising my flagging spirits with a simple word or glance. To her, this book is dedicated.

I should also add a word to our daughter Kimberly Blair. When she came into our lives, this book was nearly complete. It will be several years before she will understand its meaning and the effort that went into it. I do, however, hope that she will come to value books and the knowledge which they hold because my next one will be for her.

March 3, 1987                                    Edward F. Haas
River Ridge, Louisiana

# POLITICAL LEADERSHIP IN A SOUTHERN CITY
New Orleans in the Progressive Era,
1896-1902

# I

# Political Legacy

During the late nineteenth century, New Orleans was a city in the throes of social change. In 1870, the South's largest urban center boasted a population of 191,418. Three decades later, the figure stood at 287,104, a growth rate of nearly fifty percent. This substantial population increase derived mainly from foreign and domestic immigration as well as municipal annexations in 1870 (Jefferson City and Algiers) and in 1874 (Carrollton).[1]

An expanding populace, however, was not the only contributor to urban disarray. The racial and ethnic diversity that characterized antebellum New Orleans continued into the post-Civil War era. At the turn of the century, the federal census revealed that 77,714 black people, approximately twenty-seven percent of the total population, lived in the Crescent City. Local observers, however, contended that approximately 90,000 people was probably a more accurate figure. The black community in New Orleans, furthermore, was hardly monolithic. Among the black residents were "Creoles of color," descendants of antebellum free blacks who often spoke French, held comfortable amounts of wealth and validly claimed white ancestry. Members of this group consciously stayed apart from the more numerous former slaves and their children who generally had darker complexions and enjoyed fewer financial and educational advantages.[2]

---

1.  Bayrd Still, *Urban America: A History with Documents* (Boston, 1974), pp. 211, 265; Federal Writers' Project, *The WPA Guide to New Orleans* (Boston, 1938), p. 34; Pierce F. Lewis, *New Orleans: The Making of an Urban Landscape* (Cambridge, 1976), p. 57; Wilton P. Ledet, "The History of the City of Carrollton," *Louisiana Historical Quarterly,* XXI (January 1938), p. 276.

2.  William Ivy Hair, *Carnival of Fury: Robert Charles and the New Orleans Race Riot of 1900* (Baton Rouge, 1976), pp. 70-71; David C. Rankin, "The Im-

The South's largest port, unlike most other cities in the region, additionally had a significant immigrant population. In 1900, 10.6 percent of all local inhabitants were originally from abroad. Germans (3.0 percent) comprised the largest foreign-born group. Italians (2.0 percent), members of the new wave of immigration, ranked second. The Irish (1.9 percent) were third and the French (1.5 percent) were fourth. There were, of course, also many first-generation Americans who descended from the immigrant contingents in New Orleans and shared with their immediate forebears the trials of assimilation.[3]

The Crescent City was undeniably a crowded metropolis. The steady arrival of newcomers and the confining natural geography of the urban site caused more and more people to pack into the neighborhoods adjacent to the levees on the east bank of the Mississippi River. Whites, blacks and immigrants found themselves cheek by jowl. In New Orleans, the melting pot at times resembled a pressure cooker.[4]

During the late nineteenth century, population growth, urban crowding, ethnic rivalry and racial friction in the Crescent City awakened socioeconomic tensions that manifested themselves in acts of violence. On March 14, 1891, a mob of local citizens stormed Orleans Parish Prison and shot, hanged and clubbed to death eleven Italian prisoners after a jury had failed to convict nine of the men in the murder of Chief of Police David Hennessy. Two of the victims had not yet gone to trial.[5] In the fall of 1894 and again in the spring of 1895, violence erupted on the city wharves when

---

pact of the Civil War on the Free Colored Community of New Orleans," *Perspectives in American History*, XI (1977-1978), pp. 377-416; Dale A. Somers, "Black and White in New Orleans: A Study in Urban Race Relations, 1865-1900," *Journal of Southern History*, XL (February 1974), pp. 21-22.

3. Still, *Urban America*, p. 265; Lewis, *New Orleans*, p. 57.
4. Lewis, *New Orleans*, pp. 57-59.
5. Humbert S. Nelli, *The Business of Crime: Italians and Syndicate Crime in the United States* (New York, 1976), pp. 56-64; Joy Jackson, *New Orleans in the Gilded Age: Politics and Urban Progress, 1880-1896* (Baton Rouge, 1969), pp. 247-253.

British cotton shippers replaced white screwmen with blacks who worked for lower wages. During the second disturbance, Governor Murphy J. Foster had to summon troops to restore order.[6] Five years later, in July 1900, a dispute between New Orleans police and Robert Charles, a young black man from Copiah County, Mississippi, who espoused the back-to-Africa movement, precipitated a bloody race riot.[7]

This proclivity for violence in New Orleans society, though evident in the period before the Civil War, intensified significantly during the difficult days of Reconstruction, a disquieting time that pitted white against black and Democrat against Republican. One legacy of this perplexing era was an enormous municipal debt that burdened local government and undermined public services.[8] Another legacy was an unhealthy tolerance of governmental corruption.[9] A third—and perhaps the most important for future political development in the city—was a tightly knit Democratic urban machine that sanctioned electoral fraud and physical violence as legitimate means to manipulate politics.[10] Despite the prevalence of public dishonesty and political violence in antebellum New Orleans, these trends attained new levels of acceptance during Reconstruction.[11]

At the center of Reconstruction conflict was the Democrats' intent to maintain at all costs white supremacy in Louisiana. When on July 30, 1866, the Unionist delegates to the Constitutional Convention of 1864 attempted to reconvene the assembly in New Orleans and amend fundamen-

6. Jackson, *New Orleans in the Gilded Age*, 230; Somers, "Black and White in New Orleans," pp. 38-39.
7. Hair, *Carnival of Fury, passim.*
8. Jackson, *New Orleans in the Gilded Age*, p. 48; Wayne M. Everard, "Bourbon City: New Orleans, 1878-1900," *Louisiana Studies*, XI (Fall 1972), p. 243.
9. Joe Gray Taylor, *Louisiana: A Bicentennial History* (New York, 1976), p. 114.
10. John Smith Kendall, *History of New Orleans*, 3 vols. (Chicago, 1922), I, 445-446.
11. Taylor, *Louisiana: A Bicentennial History*, p. 114.

tal state law to include black suffrage, police fired into a group of marching freedmen. A virtual slaughter ensued. General Philip Sheridan later remarked: "It was no riot; it was an absolute massacre by the police . . . it was murder which the Mayor [John T. Monroe] and the police perpetrated without the shadow of necessity."[12]

Congress answered this Democratic challenge with the inauguration of military rule in the South. A new Federal policy successfully removed former Confederates from both public office and voter rolls and advanced the cause of black and white Republicans in Louisiana. In 1868, this radical program called for the framing of a more liberal state constitution that led directly to the election of Governor Henry Clay Warmoth, a Republican from Illinois who had served in the Union Army during the Civil War.[13]

Crescent City Democrats realized quickly that they must augment their tactical violence with strong political organization. Preparing for the municipal elections of 1868, members of the Chalmette Club, an uptown men's group that [in 1873] would merge with the exclusive Boston Club, created a secret society known as the Crescent City Democratic Club. This organization avidly endorsed white Democratic rule in Louisiana and opposed the Republicans' reign. Over the next six years, the group adopted quasi-military procedures and sporadically worked for the Democratic cause in New Orleans.[14]

In April 1874, the White League appeared in Opelousas. The organization, a paramilitary society, advocated the union of all white people in the state and condoned the use

12.    Charles L. Dufour, *Ten Flags in the Wind: The Story of Louisiana* (New York, 1967), pp. 181-184. See also Taylor, *Louisiana: A Bicentennial History,* pp. 104-105.
13.    Joe Gray Taylor, *Louisiana Reconstructed, 1863-1877* (Baton Rouge, 1974), pp. 114-161.
14.    Walter Prichard, ed., "The Origin and Activities of the 'White League' in New Orleans (Reminiscences of a Participant in the Movement)," *Louisiana Historical Quarterly,* XXIII (April 1940), pp. 528-532; Taylor, *Louisiana Reconstructed,* p. 284; Stuart O. Landry, *History of the Boston Club* (New Orleans, 1938), pp. 28, 109-113.

of force to advance Democratic goals. New units soon took root throughout the state. In New Orleans, several principal members of the Crescent City Democratic Club favored affiliation with the growing paramilitary group. On July 1, 1874, despite some vocal opposition, the Crescent City Democratic Club formally changed its name to the Crescent City White League. Leaders in the reorganization effort were Fred N. Ogden, former president of the Chalmette Club, and F. R. Southmayd. On July 2, 1874, the New Orleans *Daily Picayune* published the new group's platform. After decrying the "execrable oligarchy of the most ignorant and profligate negroes [*sic*], leagued with the most dangerous class of rapacious whites, the scum of society," the White League declared its "fixed determination . . . to maintain our own legal rights by all means that may become necessary for that purpose, and to preserve them at all hazards."[15] On September 14, 1874, this shift toward more stringent Democratic action culminated in a pitched battle between the White League and a combined force of black militia and Metropolitan Police, military arms of the Republican regime, at Liberty Place near the foot of Canal Street. Although the encounter in downtown New Orleans produced few immediate results, it became in subsequent decades a rallying point for white supremacy and the Democratic party.[16]

During the remaining years of Reconstruction in the Crescent City, detachments of the White League managed the local Democratic electoral machinery. The organization that they erected bore the qualities of a finely tuned urban political apparatus. In each municipal ward, there existed a "mother" club whose president became the ward boss. This leader commonly gained power "by dint of personal cour-

15. Quoted in Thomas Ewing Dabney, *One Hundred Great Years: The Story of the Times-Picayune from Its Founding to 1940* (Baton Rouge, 1944), p. 230. See also Taylor, *Louisiana Reconstructed*, p. 284; Landry, *History of the Boston Club*, pp. 109-113; Kendall, *History of New Orleans*, I, 359-361.
16. Taylor, *Louisiana: A Bicentennial History*, pp. 132-137; Jackson, *New Orleans in the Gilded Age*, pp. 28-37; Everard, "Bourbon City," p. 245.

age, brute strength or lack of principle." His ability to de-
liver his ward's votes to the Democratic columns insured his
continued position of importance among the state and local
political chieftains who sought white rule. The ward leader
garnered the votes of his district by granting favors and by
supplying his constituents' needs. Neighborhood residents
soon learned that the head of the Democratic ward club was
a ready and able source of aid in virtually all matters. They
also discovered that firm adherence to the Democratic ticket
constituted the proper payment for these useful benefits.
Journalist and historian John Smith Kendall stated: "It was
a system which remorselessly capitalized good fellow-
ship."[17]

When the withdrawal of Federal troops in 1877 ended Reconstruction in Louisiana, this Democratic electoral machinery remained in place. Democratic ward bosses continued to use their influence over voters and the mandatory
white supremacy to control the local party organization. In
their hands, the Democratic organization became a formidable local group that closely resembled in membership and
tactics the urban political machines of the North. Its foremost backers included the working classes, immigrants and
(until their disfranchisement in 1898) subordinate blacks.
Patronage and political favors were still the primary devices
for controlling the vote, but, when these tools failed, the
Democrats often resorted to violence and to election fraud.
New Orleans Democrats also established alliances with rural elements of the party that increased their patronage possibilities and extended their power beyond the Crescent
City. The New Orleans machine indeed became an integral
part of the conservative oligarchy that dominated state politics in the late nineteenth century. Other components of this
Democratic political amalgam included the big planters, the
agents of the state convict-lease system and the Louisiana
Lottery Company, a powerful gambling concern that held a

17.   Kendall, *History of New Orleans*, I, 387, 445-447.

government monopoly and maintained substantial financial resources.[18]

Several New Orleanians who strongly endorsed the concept of white superiority, however, opposed the direction that the local Democratic organization was taking. These men, including numerous veterans of Liberty Place and many prominent business and professional leaders, believed that the party's highly effective electoral mechanism was only a weapon of expediency in the battle against the Republicans and their black allies. With the end of Reconstruction, these individuals saw no further need for a strong political organization that frequently used fraud and violence to obtain voter support. They advocated a swift return to popular rule and fair elections. When it became apparent that the ward and precinct bosses were subverting the Democratic organization to enhance their own power and position, several leading citizens loudly announced their disapproval.[19]

In the municipal elections of 1878, splits within the Democratic ranks were already evident. When the Democratic-Conservatives—or Regular Democrats, as they came to be called—entered a slate of candidates for public office, an independent Democratic faction that adopted the name, Citizens' Conservative Movement, nominated a rival ticket. Regular Democratic candidates, particularly those whose name appeared on both tickets, immediately repudiated the new group and rejected its endorsement. The Citizens-Tax-payers-Workingmen party, another independent organization, also advanced a list of nominees. All three slates included former members of the White League who had served during the Battle of Liberty Place.[20]

18. Jackson, *New Orleans in the Gilded Age*, pp. 28-37; Taylor, *Louisiana: A Bicentennial History*, pp. 132-137; William Ivy Hair, *Bourbonism and Agrarian Protest: Louisiana Politics, 1877-1900* (Baton Rouge, 1969), pp. 14-33; Everard, "Bourbon City," p. 248.

19. Kendall, *History of New Orleans*, I, 446; Jackson, *New Orleans in the Gilded Age*, pp. 34-37.

20. Kendall, *History of New Orleans*, I, 409-412; New Orleans *Daily Picayune*, April 2, 1896.

Subsequent political contests solidified these factions. The Regulars continued to use their tightly structured ward and precinct organizations to win elections and retain governmental power. Members of the local commercial and professional elite, however, responded to these activities with a steady wave of opposition. Viewing themselves as conservative reformers who represented the true ideals of the Battle of Liberty Place, these leaders generally abhorred the political practices of the Regular Democrats. The reformers, employing names such as the Committee of One Hundred, the Young Men's Democratic Association and the Anti-Lottery League in different campaigns, consistently advocated alterations in local governmental institutions as a means to eliminate political corruption and to win election to public office (See Figure 1).

Although the reformers managed to carry a few municipal elections, they were usually unable to take advantage of their success at the polls. After each campaign, their electoral organizations tended to fragment. The reformers were essentially political amateurs who devoted most of their energies to their business and professional pursuits. For them, politics was largely an avocation. Democratic ward and precinct bosses, however, were professional politicians whose very livelihoods rested upon their ability to sway voters. Occasional disputes among machine leaders and the willingness of some reformers to enter opportunistic alignments with the still potent Republican party and splinter groups such as the Greenback and Populist parties, nonetheless, contributed to several good government victories during the era.[21]

Perhaps the most notable of these triumphs came in 1896 when the Citizens' League exploited a Republican-Populist coalition, public outrage over municipal corruption and conflict within the machine ranks to soundly defeat the

---

21.   Jackson, *New Orleans in the Gilded Age*, pp. 34-39. See also John R. Kemp, ed., *Martin Behrman of New Orleans: Memoirs of a City Boss* (Baton Rouge, 1977), pp. 59-61.

Regular Democrats. Many reformers argued confidently that this election signaled an end to machine rule in the Crescent City. They believed that a fresh new day in municipal government would soon appear.[22]

22.   Jackson, *New Orleans in the Gilded Age*, pp. 312-316; Raymond O. Nussbaum, "'The Ring Is Smashed!': The New Orleans Municipal Election of 1896," *Louisiana History*, XVII (Summer 1976), pp. 283-297; Everard, "Bourbon City," p. 250.

# II

# John Fitzpatrick and the Politics of Continuity

"The Ring is smashed!" announced the New Orleans *Daily Picayune* on April 22, 1896.[1] The previous day, Regular Democracy had suffered a stinging defeat at the polls. New Orleanians had literally voted the rascals out and given their support to the Citizens' League, a self-styled reform group that represented financially and socially prominent citizens. The success of the Citizens' League in local elections was nearly complete. Walter C. Flower, the reform candidate for mayor, to cite a major example, lost only two of seventeen wards to Congressman Charles F. Buck, the Regulars' nominee. In secondary municipal contests, the reform ticket fared equally well. Few Regular candidates won election.[2] Amid the heady aftermath of overwhelming victory, the *Daily Picayune,* a leading reform organ, proclaimed the "beginning of a new era in the political conduct of this city." The newspaper promised "a movement to reorganize the government of the city upon a system which will take away from a gang or clique of politicians the opportunity to seize upon and hold as prey the offices, the money and the public franchises which belong to the people." On April 25, 1896, the *Daily Picayune* stated: "The broken ring should be buried and forgotten."[3]

For the reformers, the triumph culminated a lengthy struggle that extended back to the turbulent era of Recon-

1.   *Daily Picayune*, April 22, 1896.
2.   Jackson, *New Orleans in the Gilded Age*, pp. 312-316: Nussbaum, "New Orleans Municipal Election of 1896," pp. 294-295. See also Everard, "Bourbon City," p. 250; George M. Reynolds, *Machine Politics in New Orleans, 1897-1926* (New York, 1936), p. 33.
3.   *Daily Picayune*, April 22, 25, 1896.

struction. It also represented a worthy reward for the stead-
fastness of the good government advocates. During the late
nineteenth century, the Crescent City Democratic machine
was a formidable adversary, but it never lacked an opposition. Although the commercial and professional elite generally accepted the racial views of the Regulars, they vehe-
mently resented the disreputable tactics that the politicians
employed to obtain and to hold power. In each important
municipal election, reform-minded citizens mounted a
frontal assault upon the Ring. On several occasions, they
managed to win, but the reformers' political forces commonly exhibited little staying power. Their organizations
were prone to dissolution after the campaign. The good
government supporters, nevertheless, were persistent. Because they would frequently join with the Republicans and
with any agreeable independent parties, the reformers always constituted a threat to the Regulars. In 1896, their efforts paid off. The involvement of several Regular councilmen in a bribery scandal moved outraged New Orleanians
to favor the opposition. The depth of public anger against
machine corruption and their substantial margin of victory
convinced the reformers that the Ring was finally dead.[4]

Despite these ominous pronouncements and the intensity of the recent campaign, the Regulars accepted their defeat with remarkable good grace. Charles Buck admitted that
loyalty to the party, not any desire to become mayor, motivated his candidacy. Dennis McCarthy, the Regular nominee for commissioner of public works, was philosophical.
He contended that "such things are pure and simple politics. It is the old story of in to-day and out to-morrow." Police Commissioner C. Taylor Gauche blamed no one. He believed that "his men did all in their power, but the numbers
were against them and the numbers counted." Mayor John

4. Jackson, *New Orleans in the Gilded Age*, pp. 28-37; Taylor, *Louisiana:
A Bicentennial History*, pp. 132-137. For the racial views of the reformers,
see Henry C. Dethloff, "Populism and Reform in Louisiana," (Ph.D. dissertation, University of Missouri, 1964), p. 174.

Fitzpatrick shared these sentiments. On the day of Walter Flower's inauguration, the outgoing chief executive wore a bright smile, administered the oath of office to his successor and then quietly departed City Hall.[5]

This gracious exit reflected the former mayor's extensive political experience. An orphan who learned carpentry and joined the volunteer fire department, Fitzpatrick was an active politician in the Third Ward from the day that he could vote. In 1872, at age twenty-eight, he attained his first public office, clerk of the First District Court. Two years later, he became clerk of the Superior Criminal Court. In 1876, following an unsuccessful campaign for Orleans Parish criminal sheriff, Fitzpatrick won election to the state legislature. After two years in state service, the young politician returned to defeat Mandeville Marigny for criminal sheriff.[6] During his time in the legislature and in the sheriff's office, Fitzpatrick earned a notable reputation for opposing the Louisiana State Lottery, and he became a serious rival to the formidable Major Edward A. Burke, state treasurer and spokesman for the New Orleans gambling interests.[7]

Fitzpatrick, nonetheless, was clearly on the rise. An added political asset was his service with the Irish Rifles, a company in the Louisiana National Guard. During this association, he acquired the nickname "Captain John," that he retained until the end of his years. By 1880 Fitzpatrick was the "Big Boss of the Third Ward" and a significant figure in lo-

5. Raymond O. Nussbaum, "Progressive Politics in New Orleans, 1896-1900," (Ph.D. dissertation, Tulane University, 1974), p. 72; *Daily Picayune*, April 24, 28, 1896. See also New Orleans *Daily States*, April 22, 1896.

6. New Orleans *Item*, April 7, 8, 1919; *Daily States*, April 7, 1919; Kendall, *History of New Orleans*, II, 506. A brief biography of Fitzpatrick is included in Works Progress Administration, "Biographies of the Mayors of New Orleans" (New Orleans, 1939), 201-203. A typescript copy is available in the Louisiana Division, New Orleans Public Library. Fitzpatrick's service with the First District Court during the administration of Republican Governor William Pitt Kellogg was a source of embarrassment for him in Democratic circles throughout his long political career. See New Orleans *Times-Democrat*, October 26, 1904.

7. Jackson, *New Orleans in the Gilded Age*, pp. 119-120. For the Fitzpatrick-Burke rivalry, see also *Item*, April 8, 1919.

cal Democratic circles. Bernard Shields, a veteran politico, later recalled that Captain John was one of the "Big Four" who dominated city politics in the 1880s. The others were Patrick Mealey of the First Ward, the perennial commissioner of police and public buildings, Robert C. Davey of the Second Ward and Tom Duffy of the Fourth Ward. Shields recollected, "Nothing was ever done unless those four gave it their sanction, and they exercised entire control of the political machine in those days."[8]

Advancement in city government accompanied Fitzpatrick's growing political stature. In 1880 he was a successful candidate for administrator of improvements despite the election of Joseph Shakspeare, a reform mayor. Two years later, Captain John became commissioner of public works under a new city charter and remained in this post throughout the administrations of Mayors William J. Behan and J. V. Guillotte. During his six years with the Department of Public Works, a lush source of patronage, Fitzpatrick enhanced his political position. He cleverly spent every available penny in his budget to hire needy workers, primarily Irish-Americans, who responded with a fierce loyalty to the Democratic machine. The *Mascot*, a critic of the Regulars, noted that these Irishmen "seem to think God made the Democratic party as immaculate and infallible as the Blessed Virgin Mary. They would stand up and vote the Democratic ticket straight if the devil and all his angels were at the hellm [sic]." The independent journal further contended that "the nearer the time draws towards the election, the greater becomes the enthusiasm of Johnny for arming the exiles of Erin with the shovel and pick-ax."[9]

In 1888, however, the Young Men's Democratic Association, a forerunner of the Citizens' League, defeated Captain John and his Regular cohorts in the city elections. Fitzpatrick lost his position to General P. G. T. Beauregard, the

8. *Item*, April 7, 1919; Kemp, ed., *Martin Behrman of New Orleans*, p. 20.
9. New Orleans *Mascot*, July 15, 1882. See also Jackson, *New Orleans in the Gilded Age*, pp. 37, 58, 74, 317-318; Works Progress Administration, "Biographies of the Mayors of New Orleans," p. 201.

Confederate war hero. This unexpected defeat surely rattled the Third Ward boss, but it provided a time of preparation for future achievement.[10]

During this lull in his career, Captain Fitzpatrick retained a substantial measure of popular favor. Employees in the Department of Public Works remembered his past generosity, and local labor leaders, recalling the politician's early days in the carpentry trade, remained friendly. An avid devotion to sports was another common bond with the workingmen of New Orleans. Fitzpatrick especially fancied boxing and refereed serveral important contests, including the heavyweight championship bout in 1889 between John L. Sullivan and Jake Kilrain. Captain John also enjoyed numerous social contacts. An inveterate joiner, he was active in the Elks, the Knights of Columbus, the Ancient Order of Hibernians, the United Irish League of New Orleans, the Continental Guards and the Firemen's Charitable and Benevolent Association as well as the Democratic party.[11]

By 1892 Fitzpatrick was clearly the most powerful politician in New Orleans. Three years earlier, Mayor Burke, his strongest rival, had absconded to Honduras with several hundred thousand dollars in public funds. The "Big Four," furthermore, had come apart. Tom Duffy of the Fourth Ward had drifted into semi-retirement, and Pat Mealey was dead, the victim of a saloon fight. Robert Davey was still powerful, but he preferred a secondary position. On April 11, 1892, Davey nominated Fitzpatrick for mayor, and the caucus of Regular ward bosses approved. Captain John was ready for the top prize.[12]

The campaign, however, proved to be a complex battle

10.   *Item*, April 7, 1919; New Orleans *Times-Picayune*, April 8, 1919; Jackson, *New Orleans in the Gilded Age*, p. 96. On April 6, 1914, the *Daily Picayune* and the *Times-Democrat* merged to form the New Orleans *Times-Picayune*.

11.   *Daily States*, April 7, 1919; Works Progress Administration, "Biographies of the Mayors of New Orleans," p. 202; Jackson, *New Orleans in the Gilded Age*, pp. 37-38.

12.   *Daily States*, September 15, 1897; Hair, *Bourbonism and Agrarian Protest*, p. 141; Kemp, ed., *Martin Behrman of New Orleans*, 20; Jackson, *New Orleans in the Gilded Age*, pp. 41-42, 133-134.

that featured sharp divisions among Louisiana Democrats over the lottery question. During the state nominating convention, lottery advocates endorsed the gubernatorial bid of Samuel D. McEnery, a former chief executive and state supreme court justice. Those who rejected the lottery, including several New Orleanians, extended independent support to Murphy J. Foster, a young state senator from St. Mary Parish. For Fitzpatrick and the urban machine, the situation was delicate. Although several local leaders adamantly opposed the gambling interests, the ward bosses did not wish to promote any additional disruption within their party. Seeing no reasonable alternative, they backed McEnery. Fitzpatrick, once a foe of the lottery, now sided with the gamblers.

On election day, growing disapproval of the lottery throughout the state pushed Foster to a landslide victory, but Fitzpatrick and the ward bosses used their superior organization to win in the city. The anti-lottery forces had failed to achieve complete success, and the political pot continued to stew. Several New Orleans Regulars who had fought the gamblers were reluctant to rejoin the machine. The reform faction, moreover, blamed Fitzpatrick and the ward bosses for their inability to win a total victory. From this resentment grew a bitter hatred of the new mayor and a strong desire to get even.

Governor Foster and Fitzpatrick, however, did not share this smoldering animosity. Despite their differing public stands on the lottery, both officials were loyal Democrats who wanted party unity and feared the rise of a Republican-Populist coalition. When Foster offered friendship to the New Orleans Democratic machine, Fitzpatrick accepted with a clear conscience and an eye toward political alliance.[13]

During his first two years in office, Captain Fitzpatrick

13. For a thorough discussion of the lottery fight of 1892, see Hair, *Bourbonism and Agrarian Protest*, 198-233; Jackson, *New Orleans in the Gilded Age*, pp. 11-135. Murphy Foster's loyalty to the Democratic party was overwhelming. See Sidney James Romero, Jr., "The Political Career of Murphy James Foster, Governor of Louisiana, 1892-1900," *Louisiana Historical Quarterly*, XXVIII (October 1945), pp. 1167, 1193.

advanced a credible program of public improvements and sound finance, but in 1894 irregularities surfaced. Several prominent citizens charged the city council with bribery in awarding paving and garbage contracts, constructing a municipal courthouse and granting a railway franchise. The good government advocates now saw their chance to attack the mayor and his associates. Irate reformers quickly initiated an investigation of the scandalous activities of the so-called "Boodle Council" that culminated with the indictment of ten councilmen, the city engineer and a former tax collector. Three of these men later went to prison for bribery.[14]

When Fitzpatrick expressed his loyalty to the indicted councilmen and refused to suspend them, the press directed its ire toward him. On July 23, 1894, the New Orleans *Daily States*, in an article entitled "The Den of Thieves," charged both the mayor and the council with bribery and misuse of powers. The newspaper concluded, "If we cannot send them to the penitentiary, let us impeach them and turn them out."[15] Fitzpatrick immediately denied any criminal acts and filed a libel suit for $100,000 in damages against the evening newspaper. Reformers, however, warmed to the idea of impeachment. On September 14, 1894, at their insistence, the district attorney began impeachment proceedings against Fitzpatrick. The case dragged into the following year, but the judge cleared the mayor of all charges after the prosecution failed to produce any hard evidence of misconduct. Fitzpatrick later won his libel suit against the *States* and received a nominal award of $500 damages. In two instances, Captain John had bested the reformers, but his triumphs were both personal and hollow. The Regulars were still in trouble. The *Daily Picayune* remarked that the mayor's victory in the libel suit was not "a vindication of his virtue and greatness."[16]

14. *Daily Picayune*, March 20, 1896; Kendall, *History of New Orleans*, II, 509-511; Jackson, *New Orleans and the Gilded Age*, pp. 137-142.
15. *Daily States*, July 23, 1894.
16. *Daily Picayune*, February 21, 1896; Kendall, *History of New Orleans*, II, 511-514; Jackson, *New Orleans in the Gilded Age*, pp. 142-143.

Fitzpatrick believed his vindication would come in the municipal elections of 1896. The mayor, encouraged by Councilman William J. Kane and Assistant City Attorney George Washington Flynn, seriously considered a bid for reelection, but wiser heads tabled the scheme. The Regulars drafted Congressman Buck and nominated a slate of candidates who were generally free from scandal. Despite these precautions, the Citizens' League vanquished the machine on election day.[17]

The defeat marked the low point of Fitzpatrick's political career. Several close friends contended that "he meant to get out of politics and give his attention in another channel." The *Daily Picayune* reported that Fitzpatrick was relieved to escape the limelight of public scandal and electoral disaster.[18]

Although the former mayor did not leave politics, he seemed to withdraw. On June 15, 1896, Louisiana Democrats named him to represent the state at the national party convention. After this gathering, however, Fitzpatrick drifted from sight. He was reputedly in Canada resting from politics. Some intimates suggested a rift with Governor Foster. The former mayor had supposedly asked the governor to support Clark Steen, Fitzpatrick's private secretary, for a state position, but Foster had preferred another candidate. On August 25, 1896, the *Daily States* noted, "Mr. Fitzpatrick hasn't been in Baton Rouge since and his friends say that no appointment has been made with his personal urging." Two days later, the afternoon newspaper again commented on the politician's absence. When Fitzpatrick later returned to the city, local Democrats immediately nominated him for Congress. The former mayor, however, declined the honor and endorsed General Adolph Meyer for the First District seat. He was still unsure about his plans.[19]

17. *Daily Picayune*, March 1, 1896; Kendall, *History of New Orleans*, II, 521-523.
18. *Daily Picayune*, April 24, 28, 1896.
19. *Daily Picayune*, June 16, September 13, 14, 23, 1896; *Daily States*, Au-

The prospects of the Regular Democrats appeared equally uncertain. On November 23, 1896, the *Daily States* reported a meeting of the Crescent Democratic Club, the Regulars' officially chartered organization, to be held four days later. Daniel A. Mayer, the group's secretary, stated that the meeting "has been called to vote upon a proposition to dissolve the club."[20] The turbulent years had evidently taken their toll.

At the same time, leading members of the Citizens' League, acknowledging the "ephemeral character" of past reform efforts, took steps to solidify their gains. Their primary aim was to establish a permanent political organization. On November 22, 1896, the *Daily Picayune* reported, "A constitution has been adopted, and it is understood that all wards in the city will have representatives in the governing body, while as complete a membership will be maintained as is possible." In subsequent weeks, over two hundred reformers signed an official charter, fulfilling the goal of permanency. On December 16, 1896, members selected a board of officers. Charles Janvier, a New Orleans insurance executive and former Mardi Gras king of Rex who had been a major figure in the recent municipal campaign, became president.[21] The outlook for local reformers appeared good.

Careful political observers, however, were reluctant to dismiss the Regulars. On May 30, 1896, an editorial writer for the *Daily Picayune*, using a slang expression from the current bicycling craze, commented, "The ring snake was scorched, without being killed." The Regulars, like pedestrians who experienced close encounters with reckless wheelmen, had suffered considerable psychological trauma, but the physical damage was minimal. Good government supporters also recognized the resilience of the political

---

gust 25, 27, September 6, 7, 17, 1896; Baton Rouge *Daily Advocate*, September 10, 1896.

20. *Daily States*, November 23, 1896.

21. *Daily Picayune*, November 22, 25, December 13, 17, 1896, January 11, June 25, 1897.

professionals. Citizens League spokesmen publicly hoped
that a lively reform group would force the Regulars to present better candidates.[22]

The wisdom of these remarks was soon apparent. While
the reformers applauded their early organizational
triumphs, a committee of Regular Democrats planned a res-
urrection. On December 29, 1896, the New Orleans *Times-
Democrat* announced, "A general meeting of those interested in the formation of a new Democrat Club . . . this evening at 8 o'clock. . . . ." The assembly would take place fittingly in the rooms of the defunct Crescent Democratic
Club.[23]

At the appointed hour, the politicians arrived. Peter Stifft,
an attorney and chairman of the committee on organization, presided over the gathering that the *Daily Picayune*
deemed "business-like." The newspaper stated that "those
present knew what they were about." The *New Orleans
Times-Democrat* reported that "between forty and fifty Democrats" attended the meeting. The *Daily Picayune* set the figure at "about seventy-five."

First, the assembled Democrats selected a name. Since
their intent "was the reformation of a regular Democratic
organization, on the line of the famous Tammany and Iroquois Clubs," they chose an Indian name. Following the
advice of the organizational committee, the members sifted
through several Indian names, including Natchez, Chicka-
saw, Tensas and Houmas before they decided to call their
group the Choctaw Club of Louisiana. A few dissidents argued that a more suitable name was the Jackson Democratic
Club. But Frank D. Chretien objected to the insertion of a
party designation because "the club was to have a social as
well as political feature." Others contended "that the in-

22. *Ibid.*, May 30, 1896. For the term "scorcher," see Dabney, *One Hundred Great Years*, p. 294.
23. *Times-Democrat*, December 29, 1896. The members of the committee were Peter Stifft, W. A. Kernaghan, B. T. Walshe, J. W. Frellsen, A. V.
Flotte, J. J. McCann, and W. L. Hughes. See *Daily Picayune*, December 30,
1896.

corporation of the word 'Democratic' was synonymous with failure in organizations of this character," and observed "that the Crescent Democratic and Jefferson Democratic clubs of this city proved failures, while such powerful Democratic organizations in the North as 'Tammany,' of New York, and the 'Iroquois' Club of Chicago, did not incorporate the name of the party with which they were so intimately identified in the official name of the organization." The *Daily Picayune* later stated that the Choctaw Club was "an imitation Tammany association." The choice of a name also produced a rare diversion in an otherwise sober meeting. When the members made their final selection, John Bach, a stockbroker, rushed into the hall with a feather duster stuck in the back of his shirt and gave a Choctaw warwhoop.[24]

The embryonic Choctaws next adopted a charter which maintained "that the welfare of the Country, and the continual prosperity of its institutions require for their preservation that the policy and character of the Government shall be determined and guided by the principles of the Democratic Party" and sought "to add to the organized strength of the Democratic Party in the State of Louisiana. . . ." The avowed "objects and purposes" of the organizations were "To uphold and advance Democratic principles . . ."; "To promote harmony, enjoyment and literary improvement . . ."; and "To provide the conveniences of a Club House."[25] The charter also established a board of governors and divided the membership into three categories: resident, nonresident and life members. Another charter provision called for the creation of a permanent committee on organization that would "act and pass upon all matters affecting the honor, preservation and integrity of the Democratic Party in this State." After a lengthy discussion, those in atten-

24. *Times-Democrat*, December 30, 1896; *Daily Picayune*, December 30, 1896, January 2, 1897.
25. See Kemp, ed., *Martin Behrman of New Orleans*, p. 344; *Item*, November 2, 1922.

dance agreed that Choctaws in each of the seventeen wards of New Orleans would elect a representative to the committee and that these selections would be subject to the ratification of the members-at-large.[26]

The remainder of the proceedings went smoothly. The members approved the first board of governors and agreed that this body would elect a president, vice-president and secretary-treasurer when the charter of the organization became official.[27] Although there was no actual balloting, everyone understood that William A. Kernaghan, a real estate agent, would become the first president of the Choctaw Club, if he wanted the post. At the close of the meeting, several members signed the new charter, but Peter Stifft announced that the document would be available later at his law office for additional signatures.[28]

Martin Behrman, who attended the initial meeting, later recalled that there were 138 charter members of the Choctaw Club. In May 1902 a special edition of *Club Life* that featured the organization also cited this number.[29] The official document that Peter Stifft notarized and William Ardell witnessed, however, listed ninety-two signatures. Eighty-four signees were New Orleanians and eight were nonresidents.[30] Behrman and the journal of "southern clubdom" were evidently mistaken, or they included Choctaws who attended the first meeting and did not sign the charter.[31]

26.  *Times-Democrat*, December 30, 1896; *Daily Picayune*, December 30, 1896.
27.  The members of the first board of governors were W. A. Kernaghan, P. A. Capdau, John J. Frawley, Joseph Frellsen, B. T. Walshe, Peter Stifft, Frank D. Chretien, L. R. Garcia and Charles Dickson.
28.  *Daily Picayune*, December 30, 1896; *Times-Democrat*, December 30, 1896.
29.  *Item*, November 2, 1922; "The Choctaw Club of Louisiana," *Club Life*, Special Edition (May 1902), p. 1.
30.  Charter of the Choctaw Club of Louisiana, March 12, 1897, Recorder of Mortgages, Civil District Court, New Orleans, Louisiana. The official charter omitted one name, A. L. Bourgeois, that was on the copy of the document in Peter Stifft's notarial files. See Peter Stifft, Notarial Acts 1-108, May 1894-November 1897, Orleans Parish Notarial Archives.
31.  Clark Steen was one such person. *Daily Picayune*, December 30, 1896.

Although the actual number of early members remained uncertain, the political lineage of those who signed the document was clear. The Choctaws were veterans of the Democratic machine. Thirty-nine charter members had held public office on the municipal, parish and state level during Regular Democratic administrations before 1896. Six had been members of the Democratic State Central Committee from Orleans Parish in January 1896. Six belonged to the caucus of New Orleans ward leaders that had selected the Regular ticket for the city elections of 1896. Ten, including Peter Stifft, had been candidates on that ticket.[32]

Many of these politicos could trace their antecedents directly to the Crescent Democratic Club. Daniel A. Mayer, for instance, had been secretary of the dissolved organization. Robert S. Landry had been the assistant secretary and would become the first secretary-treasurer of the Choctaw Club. The first governing board of the Crescent Democratic Club, moreover, included future Choctaws C. Taylor Gauche, O. A. Trezevant and John Bach (he of the warwhoop).[33] On September 2, 1932, a writer in a Regular Democratic brochure reminisced, "The Choctaw Club was born from the Crescent Democratic Club, which was formed in 1891."[34]

Several charter members, however, boasted political roots that extended even farther into the Democratic past. Blayney Walshe, who participated in the organizational planning of the Choctaw Club, signed the charter and became a member of the first board of governors, provided an example of lengthy political prominence. Before he became tax

32. *Ibid.*, January 14, April 6, 16, 1896.
33. See "Choctaw Club," 1; *Daily States*, November 23, 1896; Lon Soards. *Soards' New Orleans City Directory for 1896* (New Orleans, 1896), p. 487. Hereinafter cited as *Soards*, date, page number. See also Charter of the Crescent Democratic Club, May 23, 1891, Recorder of Mortgages, Civil District Court, New Orleans, Louisiana.
34. Souvenir Program, Choctaw Club of Louisiana, Choctaw Day, Pontchartrain Beach, September 2, 1932. This program is available in the Louisiana Historical Center, Louisiana State Museum, New Orleans, Louisiana. See also *Thirty-Five Years of Progress in New Orleans . . .* (New Orleans, n. d.), p. 69.

collector for the Sixth District, Walshe served as administrator of finance, treasurer and city councilman in the administrations of Joseph Shakspeare, W. J. Behan and J. V.
Guillotte, respectively. Joseph D. Taylor was city notary
from 1882 until the inauguration of Mayor Flower. Victor
Mauberret, Thomas J. Carey and Edward S. Maunsell were
councilmen during the Guillotte years.[35] Ferdinand Dudenhefer, one of the few victorious Regulars in 1896, had represented the Ninth Ward of New Orleans in the state legislature since 1879.[36]

Other Choctaws who had not held public posts, nonetheless, pursued careers that related closely to governmental affairs and politics. Seven were lawyers. Frank P. Mullen
and Brainard Rorison, a nonresident member, represented
the Barber Asphalt Paving Company. Four others were
contractors and manufacturers of building materials. Edward A. Brandao was a printer and Charles W. Corson, a
stationer. In a day when saloons were political hot beds, H.
C. Ramos, inventor of the famed Ramos Gin Fizz, was one
of six bar keepers. Gustave Oertling was the secretary-treasurer of the Jackson Brewing Company.

The influence of John Fitzpatrick, the deposed mayor, was
also in evidence among the charter members. C. Taylor
Gauche had been commissioner of police and public buildings in the Fitzpatrick administration. Remy Klock had been
criminal sheriff. Frank E. Bishop and John T. Brady had
worked as tax clerks in the city treasurer's office. William
Nelson and Pierre A. Fortier had been constables of the First
and Second City Courts, respectively. Charles Dickson,
William J. Kane, Charles Noel, Daniel A. Mayer and George
W. Foster had been members of the "Boodle Council." Martin Behrman and Thomas J. Moulin had been committee
clerks for the council. George Washington Flynn had been
assistant city attorney.[37] Clark Steen, Captain John's secre-

35.  Jackson, *New Orleans in the Gilded Age*, 323-327; *Soards, 1898*, p. 836.
36.  "Choctaw Club," 48.
37.  *Soards, 1896*, pp. 105, 119, 139, 247, 313, 317, 337, 467, 601, 614, 621;
Jackson, *New Orleans in the Gilded Age*, p. 327.

tary, did not sign the Choctaw charter, but he was a vocal participant in the first meeting.[38]

Fitzpatrick was not a charter member of the organization nor was he present at the initial gathering. On December 29, 1986, the former urban chief executive chose instead to attend a function for the St. Mary's Orphan Asylum, his favorite charity. Captain John, however, did send his regrets and expressed his approval of the club, a hearty endorsement that masked the true magnitude of his involvement. At the time of his death in 1919, obituaries in the *Times-Picayune*, *Daily States* and *Item* stated that Fitzpatrick, the most powerful politician of his generation, was the organizer and founder of the Choctaw Club. Shortly after the organization's first meeting, he became its leader and a life member.[39]

Murphy Foster supported the Choctaw Club enthusiastically. The governor, fearing the Citizens' League's open association with Populists and Republicans, supplied the Choctaws with patronage, the basic sustenance of all political machines. Regular bosses, freshly ousted from municipal jobs, received lucrative appointments in state government.[40] In January 1897, Foster named three charter members of the Choctaw Club and two other veteran Regulars to assessorships in Orleans Parish.[41] Remy Klock became a state coal gauger. Clark Steen and William A. Kernaghan obtained posts with the board of commissioners for the port of New Orleans. Walter C. Murphy became superintendent of the New Basin Canal Board, a state appointment, and promptly named several machine associates to

38.  *Daily Picayune*, December 30, 1896.

39.  *Ibid.; Item*, April 7, 1919, November 2, 1922; *Times-Picayune*, April 8, 1919; *Daily States*, April 7, 8, 1919.

40.  *Times-Democrat*, September 9, 1899. For the Citizens' League's alliance with the Republicans and Populists, see Jackson, *New Orleans in the Gilded Age*, 312-316. See also Everard, "Bourbon City," p. 250.

41.  *Times-Democrat*, January 14, 1897. The Choctaws were C. Taylor Gauche, Martin Behrman and O. A. Trezevant; the Regulars were Joseph Hirn and Henry B. McMurray who both later joined the political club. See "Choctaw Club," 8-9. See also *Daily Advocate*, January 9, 1897.

subordinate positions with his agency. Thanks to Governor Foster, New Orleans Regular Democrats could reward their loyal members with jobs in the state administration.[42]

On May 1, 1897, President Kernaghan, Vice-President B. T. Walshe and Secretary-Treasurer Landry presided over the formal opening of the Choctaw Club. The atmosphere was festive, but the assembled politicos were in earnest when they pledged themselves to advance the Democratic party in Louisiana. Frank Chretien declared that the object of the Choctaw Club was to unite Louisiana Democrats. Charles Buck expressed joy "to see the Democracy of New Orleans come together for the purpose of consultation and deliberation." He further stated that the Choctaw Club "was not a place for red fire and stage thunder, but serious and staid purpose." The Choctaws should "let the spirit of harmony prevail. . . ." John Fitzpatrick observed that the "principle of the club was to promote Democratic doctrine throughout the state and the city as well." With an obvious reference to the black suffrage question, Charles T. Madison contended the Choctaw tribe had always been loyal friends of the white man. He concluded that the Choctaws "were a true and steadfast set of men."[43]

Fitzpatrick and the New Orleans Regulars were in the vanguard of those who advocated disfranchising black voters. They, like most Democrats, openly endorsed the constitutional convention that the legislature had called to meet in February 1898 and contended that blacks constituted a corrupting influence in state politics.[44] Frank Chretien even suggested that "there was a possibility of the flag of reconstruction being raised again." Many New Orleans Democrats, furthermore, believed that Republicans had manipulated black votes to achieve victory for the Citizens' League

42. *Daily Picayune,* August 28, September 1, 3, 1896; *Times-Democrat,* January 14, 1897; *Soards, 1897,* p. 483; *Soards, 1898,* p. 466.
43. *Daily Picayune,* May 2, 1897; *Times-Democrat,* May 2, 1897.
44. *Daily Picayune,* August 2, 26, 29, October 9, November 25, 1897; *Times-Democrat,* August 1, 1897.

in 1896.[45] On November 24, 1897, Fitzpatrick, Remy Klock and George Washington Flynn urged Democrats in the Third Ward to register to vote so that suffrage could be withheld from "a certain worthless class." Another speaker said, "Let the ballots speak with intelligence and with knowledge by men who know how to read and write." The former mayor and criminal sheriff also stressed the need for Democratic unity.[46]

With this plea for Democratic solidarity, patronage from the state administration and sound ward organizations, the Choctaws increased their ranks and dominated the Orleans delegation to the constitutional convention. An expanding membership forced the club to seek new, larger quarters.[47] On December 8, 1897, two days after the nominations of delegates to the constitutional convention, the *Daily Picayune* complained, "The bosses control the nominations. They put up themselves or their henchmen as candidates against all opposition, and the objectionable persons are elected because nobody dares to vote against the party's candidates." On January 11, 1898, Crescent City voters approved the constitutional convention and elected delegates of a decidedly Regular bent. Among the Orleans representatives were Choctaw bosses Fitzpatrick, Flynn, Sidney March, Ferdinand Dudenhefer, Robert Ewing and Martin Behrman. Only Dr. H. Dickson Bruns, a Citizens' League leader and delegate-at-large, and John St. Paul, another Citizens' League representative, did not fit the mold.[48]

Preparations for the constitutional convention coincided with Fitzpatrick's official rise in the Choctaw Club. On January 12, 1898, club members elected the former mayor to

45. *Daily Picayune*, May 2, 1897; Jackson, *New Orleans in the Gilded Age*, pp. 312-316; Kemp, ed., *Martin Behrman of New Orleans*, pp. 38-40.
46. *Daily Picayune*, November 25, 1897.
47. "Choctaw Club," p. 1.
48. *Daily Picayune*, December 7, 8, 1897, January 12, 1898. For the calls for Democratic unity, see *Times-Democrat*, January 10, 12, 1898; *Daily Picayune*, December 12, 16, 1897. See also Nussbaum, "Progressive Politics in New Orleans," p. 184: Raynolds, *Machine Politics*, p. 34.

their new board of governors. One week later, the board named him president.[49] On February 6, 1898, a group of convention delegates, meeting at the Choctaw Club, also recognized the leadership ability of the Crescent City politico and appointed him to a committee on organization for the upcoming conclave.[50] The time was ripe for Fitzpatrick and the New Orleans machine to display their political power in Louisiana's foremost public arena, the state constitutional convention.

On February 8, 1898, the convention began at Tulane Hall in New Orleans.[51] Crescent City attorney E. B. Kruttschnitt, chairman of the Democratic State Central Committee, was the unanimous choice for convention president. Robert S. Landry of the Choctaw Club became secretary. The most influential delegate, however, was John Fitzpatrick. He belonged to the committee on organization and rules and the vital committee on suffrage and elections. The former mayor also chaired the powerful committee on the affairs of the city of New Orleans and served on the committee that distributed convention patronage favors among the various districts around the state.[52]

Throughout the convention, Fitzpatrick and the machine delegates vigorously backed constitutional provisions that benefited the Regular organization in New Orleans. Although the disfranchisement of the black voter was a foregone conclusion, the related questions of immigrant balloting and the poll tax were still sensitive. Under the Louisiana constitution of 1879 immigrants who professed an intent to become American citizens could vote in state elections. Ed-

49. "Choctaw Club," p. 1.
50. *Times-Democrat*, February 7, 1898.
51. For a thorough examination of the constitutional convention of 1898, see Hair, *Bourbonism and Agrarian Protest*, pp. 268-279; J. Morgan Kousser, *The Shaping of Southern Politics: Suffrage Restriction and the Establishment of the One-Party South, 1880-1910* (New Haven, 1974), pp. 152-165; Matthew J. Schott, "Progressives Against Democracy: Electoral Reform in Louisiana, 1894-1921," *Louisiana History*, XX (Summer 1979), pp. 253-255.
52. *Daily Picayune*, February 9, 12, 1898; *Times-Democrat*, February 9, 10, 1898; Nussbaum, "Progressive Politics in New Orleans," p. 184.

ucational requirements that promised to disfranchise blacks, however, also threatened those immigrants who did not speak English. In special jeopardy was the Italian voter, a mainstay of machine support. To resolve this difficulty, the committee on suffrage proposed that all immigrants who became naturalized citizens before January 1, 1898, regardless of literacy, should have the right to vote. A hostile press responded swiftly to this constitutional stratagem with charges that the plan created a "Privileged Dago" voter and insulted native citizens who had to meet educational and property qualifications. On May 15, 1898, the *Times-Democrat* attributed the scheme "to the subtle but potent influence of the bosses, who have maintained their political strength and carried primaries and elections through the use of these [immigrant] voters." The newspaper went on to forecast "trouble at the polls" in the next city elections. Convention delegates, nonetheless, solidly approved the clause.[53]

Fitzpatrick and the Regular Democrats also fought the poll tax that H. Dickson Bruns and several rural representatives favored. Although the exclusion levy had worked well in other southern states, the tax perplexed ward politicians who shepherded literally hundreds of voters to the polls. The *Daily Picayune* explained, "The New Orleans ward bosses are unalterably opposed to a poll tax, because they know it means their requiem as political leaders. The element which is invariably found in their wake will not put up the necessary dollar or two themselves, and it could cost a fortune to any ward leader to attempt to supply the wherewith."[54] The *Daily States* contended that the Regulars "will sacrifice the best interests of the city and the welfare of the whole State to secure the franchise to the riffraff and

53. *Daily Picayune*, February 16, March 3, 4, 7, 8, 25, 26, 1898; *Times-Democrat*, March 3, 5, 6, 8, 11, 16, 25, 1898; *Daily States*, March 25, 1898; George E. Cunningham, "The Italian, a Hinderance to White Solidarity in Louisiana," *Journal of Negro History*, L (January 1965), pp. 22-36.
54. *Daily Picayune*, March 2, 3, 10, 11, 1898. See also *Times-Democrat*, March 3, 1898.

the hoodlum, who constitute their support."[55] After an im-
passioned and sometimes confusing discussion, the convention delegates accepted the poll tax, but they agreed to
implement the levy only after the forthcoming municipal
elections in New Orleans that the Choctaws intended to
win.[56] The *Daily States* later commented, "Nearly every man
in the body realizes that it was a settlement injurious to the
city of New Orleans."[57]

In the days and weeks that followed acceptance of the
suffrage compromises, Fitzpatrick, in the opinion of the New
Orleans *Times-Democrat*, "the arch-ringster of this city," intensified his political maneuvering and revealed the true
extent of his power.[58] To the dismay of reformers, Captain
John advocated an end to Sunday closing laws, sought to
abolish city civil service and attempted to retain simulta-
neous municipal, parochial and state elections that promoted a straight party vote. His aims, furthermore, seemed
attainable.[59] On April 23, 1898, the *Times-Democrat* stated that
Fitzpatrick and a few of his followers planned to use the
convention to "instill new life into the old ring, and help
them back into office."[60] On April 27, 1898, the *Daily Picayune* said Fitzpatrick's power over the state convention was
"complete and undisputed. His will was law."[61] The following day, the *Daily States* condemned the entire convention: "Instead of being the champion of the best interests of
Louisiana, it has become the salvation of the City Ring."[62]
On May 2, 1898, the *Times-Democrat* maintained, "Mr. Fitzpatrick is as much boss of the Constitutional Convention as

55. *Daily States*, March 3, 1898.
56. *Times-Democrat*, March 25, 1898; *Daily Picayune*, March 25, 26, 1898.
See also *Times-Democrat*, March 4, 5, 8, 9, 18, 1898.
57. *Daily States*, April 20, 1989.
58. *Times-Democrat*, April 25, 1898.
59. *Ibid.*, April 6, 7, 1898; *Daily Picayune*, April 1, 3, 6, 7, 16, 20, 1898;
Nussbaum, "Progressive Politics in New Orleans," pp. 187-190.
60. *Times-Democrat*, April 23, 1898.
61. *Daily Picayune*, April 25, 27, 1898.
62. *Daily States*, April 28, 1898.

he was boss of the city ring. . . . It will go down in history as Fitzpatrick's convention."[63]

Newspapers in the outlying parishes echoed these views. The Lake Providence *Banner-Democrat* stated, "There are some men in it who have not been controlled by the city ring, but they were in the minority and could do nothing." The Homer *Guardian-Journal* complained, "Fitzpatrick is the political boss of New Orleans and will be in a position to have his way in the politics of the State. The surprising, as well as disgusting, part of the business is that so many of the country delegates have become his dupes, or tools."[64] The Shreveport *Caucasian* stated, "Never has there been a more humiliating spectacle, a more complete surrender to the political machine."[65]

In the concluding stages of the convention, Fitzpatrick focused on the election issue. On May 5, 1898, he upset reform efforts to establish a nonpartisan atmosphere in New Orleans politics by introducing a plan to conduct municipal and party-oriented parochial elections at the same time. Although Dr. Bruns and the good government supporters protested, the majority of delegates endorsed the measure.[66]

Fitzpatrick, however, temporarily shelved his opposition to civil service and the Sunday laws. He intended to resume these battles in the legislature.[67] On May 27, 1898, Captain John won the Regular nomination to the state house of representatives. The *Daily Picayune* commented, "Mr. Fitzpatrick was the acknowledged boss of the Constitutional Convention. If he should be elected, he may be quite as able to impress himself upon the Legislature." Two weeks later, the Third Ward leader was victorious.[68]

63. *Times-Democrat*, May 6, 1898.
64. Quoted in *Daily Picayune*, May 14, 1898.
65. Quoted in *ibid.*, May 5, 1898.
66. *Ibid.*, May 6, 7, 1898; Nussbaum, "Progressive Politics in New Orleans," pp. 188-189.
67. *Times-Democrat*, May 8, 1898; *Daily Picayune*, May 8, June 18, 1898.
68. *Daily Picayune*, May 28, June 10, 1898.

The success of the Regular Democrats contrasted sharply with the problems of the Citizens' League. Although the reformers had attempted to launch several progressive programs in New Orleans, their efforts were largely unsuccessful. The good government group, furthermore, failed to develop a strong network of ward organizations. By early 1899, fragmentation was evident. Several of the reformers had already defected to the Choctaws and others would soon follow.[69] Charles Janvier eventually resigned the presidency of the Citizens' League and vowed to retire from politics. He would later join several of his reform colleagues in the Choctaw Club.[70]

The Regular Democrats, on the other hand, showed great resilience. Despite a few factional disputes, the caucus of ward bosses remained virtually unchanged.[71] In eleven of seventeen city wards, the leaders who had selected the Regular ticket three years earlier still reigned. In two additional wards, the bosses' carefully chosen successors held control (See Table 1).[72] On August 4, 1899, the *Daily States* observed that "it is a fact that the bosses rallied after their defeat in 1888, and we learn from all this shouting that they have rallied after their defeat in 1896."[73] On August 24, 1899, the *Times-Democrat* noted that John Fitzpatrick was still "the head and front of the ring."[74] A week earlier, the newspaper had discussed the choice of candidates for the city elections and predicted that "the ring convention will be composed of dummy delegates named by the bosses—and even these delegates will not be allowed to make nominations or do anything whatever, but will only confirm the ticket agreed on in some back room of Remy Klock's by a cabal

69. Nussbaum, "Progressive Politics in New Orleans," pp. 188-189.

70. *Times-Democrat*, September 15, 1899; *Daily Picayune*, December 31, 1899; "Choctaw Club," 6-10.

71. See *Daily Picayune*, January 27, February 1, March 5, 21, 1899; *Times-Democrat*, January 27, 31, March 5, 17, 19, 21, July 5, 6, 1899.

72. *Daily Picayune*, September 9, 1899.

73. *Daily States*, August 4, 1899.

74. *Times-Democrat*, August 24, 1899.

composed of Fitzpatrick, 'Mike' Fanning, Farrell, Dudenhefer, Davey, 'Vic' Mauberret and possibly one or two others."[75]

The *Times-Democrat*, however, had overlooked John
Brewster, perennial leader of the Sixth Ward, and Alexander Pujol, the powerful successor to Alfred Barnes in the
Fifth Ward. These two men influenced the caucus decision
to nominate Paul Capdevielle for mayor. Capdevielle, a politically active businessman who had been a charter member of the Citizens' League, was not the first choice of Fitzpatrick and several other ward leaders, but the Regular
Democrats quickly closed ranks behind their nominee.
Captain John became his campaign manager.[76] The remainder of the ticket bore a definitely Regular character. Three
candidates had served on the "Boodle Council" during the
Fitzpatrick years. Five additional nominees were current
members of the machine caucus. Others including Frank
Bishop, Fred Zengel and Charles Kennedy were professional officerholders of long standing.[77]

On September 20, 1899, the *Times-Democrat* condemned
the Regular candidates and the ward leaders who selected
them. The newspaper declared, "These are the men, with
one or two exceptions, who named the ring ticket in 1892
and told us it was 'good'; who named the ring ticket in 1896
and tried to get into power again by showing that the head
of the ticket was a gentleman of high integrity and honor,
and who have named the 'ring' ticket now before us."
Throughout the campaign, the newspaper continued its assault on the Regulars and "their scandalous methods of
making nominations."[78] On October 31, 1899, the *Times-
Democrat* concentrated on Remy Klock, "boss of the Third

75. *Ibid.*, August 17, 1899.
76. *Daily Picayune*, September 10, 12, 13, 15, 16, 17, 1899; *Times-Democrat*, September 11, 12, 16, 18, 1899. Fitzpatrick briefly considered running
for mayor himself. *Daily Picayune*, September 5, 1899; *Times-Democrat*, September 26, 1899.
77. *Times-Democrat*, September 26, 1899.
78. *Ibid.*, September 20, 1899.

Ward," who "nominated himself for sheriff, just as he had done in 1892 and as he did again in 1896." The newspaper claimed that other bosses named themselves or put in puppets to represent them.[79] The next day, the New Orleans daily conceded that some of the names on the Regular Democratic ticket were new, "but the men who nominated it are the same, the men who are managing the campaign are the same, and the men who are behind the boxes or around the polls are the same. The whole ring election machinery is the same as that which the ring has used in every previous election."[80]

The opposition to this Regular phalanx was the Jackson Democratic Association, a hastily contrived reform group that drew its support from the nearly defunct Citizens' League. At the top of its ticket was Mayor Walter Flower, the incumbent who had himself briefly flirted with the Regulars. Although the "Jacks" tried desperately to develop a solid slate of candidates, their ward and precinct organizations were deficient.[81] They could not cope with the well-honed Regular Democratic machine. On November 7, 1899, New Orleans voters went to the polls and convincingly returned the Regulars to power.[82]

That evening Paul Capdevielle acknowledged the contributions of Captain Fitzpatrick in the contest. In his victory address, the mayor-elect began, "If I have been victorious in this campaign, I owe it all to . . ." when a speaker from the audience abruptly interjected, "You owe it to John Fitzpatrick." Capdevielle quickly took the cue. He continued, "Yes, I tell you that I owe it to Mr. John Fitzpatrick, the energetic, able and indefatigable chairman of the campaign committee. He has been absolutely devoted to the Democratic party and to me throughout this long and arduous campaign."[83]

79.  *Ibid.*, October 31, 1899.
80.  *Ibid.*, November 1, 1899.
81.  Nussbaum, "Progressive Politics in New Orleans," pp. 202-210.
82.  *Times-Democrat*, November 8, 1899.
83.  *Daily Picayune*, November 8, 1899.

With this victory and acclamation, Fitzpatrick achieved the vindication for his municipal administration that he had sought three years previously. The Citizens' League, not the Regular Democrats, had folded. Crescent City reformers, to use the words of Tammany boss George Washington Plunkitt, proved again to be "mornin' glories."[84] At the turn of the century, the Ring remained the prevalent faction in New Orleans politics. For the next fifty years, the Regular machine would dominate the South's largest city. Its demise, like the death of Mark Twain, had been greatly exaggerated.

84.  William L. Riordon, *Plunkitt of Tammany Hall* (New York, 1948, 1963), p. 17.

# III

# Men of Prominence and Principle: The Citizens' League of New Orleans

The pattern of reform organizations in New Orleans was familiar to local political observers. On November 21, 1896, the *Daily States* reported that after a reform movement has won an electoral battle, "the organization is allowed to lapse, and the next time a reform movement is necessary the preliminary work has to be done all over again." The Young Men's Democratic Association of 1888 constituted a classic example. The afternoon newspaper stated: "That was a reform body called suddenly into life to make war upon the ring government then in control of the city. After the election was over, however, the leaders retired and the forces went to pieces." The Regular Democrats, on the other hand, had "maintained their organization, worked steadily and quietly and four years after, in the midst of the anti-lottery campaign [,] slipped back into office because the reform element was generally disorganized."[1]

In 1896, however, the leaders of the Citizens' League hoped to end this repetitious pattern. Expressing "a strong sentiment" in favor of continuing the organization, members of the executive committee "concluded that permanent organization was advisable. . . ." They resolved "to charter the League and maintain it as a body for future political and other contests." President Charles Janvier promised to have something for the press "in the course of the next few days."[2] On November 22, 1896, the *Daily Picayune*

1. *Daily States*, November 21, 1896.
2. *Ibid.*

claimed that a constitution for the Citizens' League had been adopted.[3]

On November 13, 1896, the *Daily States* announced that the Citizens' League "is now a certainty" and published the organization's new charter. The newly formed organization's aims and objectives were to establish a library for its members and to provide more spacious quarters. The group would additionally sponsor lectures, debates and discussions of historical, social and political topics.

The charter also called for the election of a president, five vice-presidents, a secretary and a treasurer. It would be the duty of the president "within thirty (30) days after the date of his election to appoint an executive committee consisting of one (1) member selected from each ward and ten (10) members selected from the city at large." This executive committee would "have the entire control and management of the business of the 'League' and shall exercise all the powers incident to directors of corporations." This structure closely resembled the caucus of ward leaders that governed the operation of the Regular Democratic machine.

The Citizens' League, however, differed from the Regular organization in one important respect. Article V of the new charter stated, "No one shall be eligible to any office in the 'League' or Membership upon the Executive Committee who holds or is a candidate for any office bringing emoluments to the holder under the City Government." The document continued, "Acceptance by any person of any office provided for in this Charter will constitute an agreement between the said person and the 'League' that he will not be a candidate for nor accept any position of profit under the City Government within three (3) months from the date of his resignation of such office."[4] The members of the Citizens' League were clearly men of principle.

On December 16, 1896, the Citizens' League held its first

3.   *Daily Picayune*, November 22, 1896.
4.   *Daily States*, December 13, 1896. See also *ibid.*, December 19, 1896.

meeting. The assembled members elected Charles Janvier to the presidency of the organization. Janvier had led the group throughout the municipal campaign of 1896. Bernard McCloskey became first vice-president; Isaac L. Lyons, second vice-president; Paul Capdevielle, third vice-president; Isadore Hernsheim, fourth vice-president; and H. Dickson Bruns, fifth vice-president. George W. Young became treasurer and Hugh A. Bayne, secretary.[5]

Two hundred thirty-five men became charter members of the new organization. The *Daily States* contended, "All of those who have affixed their signatures to the charter are men who took a lively interest in the recent fight, and who worked day and night to have victory perch on their banners." On the list were "some of the most prominent men in the city."[6] The *Daily Picayune* reported that the Citizens' League hoped "as complete a membership will be maintained as is possible."[7] The *Daily States* predicted that "the list of members will swell from its present number to several thousand in a very short while."[8] The validity of the afternoon daily's forecast remained to be seen, but no one would doubt that the 235 men who signed the charter of the Citizens' League formed the core of the reform movement in New Orleans.

Most were native Louisianians. One hundred forty-five of the charter members (63.0 percent) had been born in the Pelican State. The majority of this native-born group were New Orleanians. One hundred eight members of the Citizens' League were born in the Crescent City (See Table 2). Several boasted long local lineages. Felix Couturie, for instance, was a member of one of the pioneer Franco-Louisiana families in New Orleans. Charles Janvier's family was one of the oldest Creole families in this State. Dr. Yves R. LeMonnier's great grandfather on his mother's side was

5. *Ibid.*, December 17, 1896.
6. *Ibid.*, December 13, 1896.
7. *Daily Picayune*, November 22, 1896.
8. *Daily States*, December 13, 1896.

General John Labutal, who commanded the militia at the battle of New Orleans. His paternal grandfather was a surgeon general under Andrew Jackson. Walter D. Denegre, a native-born Orleanian, belonged to a prominent Creole family.[9] Denegre's brother George, another native New Orleanian, was also a charter member of the Citizens' League.[10]

Many of the charter members who were native to other parts of Louisiana came to the Crescent City at an early age. Peter Clement, for example, was a native of Plaquemine, Louisiana, who moved to the metropolis when he was eight years old. Walter C. Flower was born in East Feliciana Parish. The mayor's father was a planter whose business ultimately brought him and his family to New Orleans. John M. Sherrouse was a North Louisiana native who at age seventeen decided to seek his fortune in the port city.[11]

Forty additional charter members of the Citizens' League were native southerners. Many of these men, like the Louisianians from outlying parishes, were youngsters when they arrived in the Crescent City. Isadore Hernsheim, for example, according to a Citizens' League commemorative brochure, was born in Mississippi and came to New Orleans when quite young. Dr. Quitman Kohnke was a native of Natchez, Miss., whose parents removed to the city when he was only an infant. Born in 1860, W. L. McGary was a native of Paducah, Ky. He came to the Crescent City with his parents when he was a child. William E. Uniacke was a Mississippian by birth, having been born in Summit in June, 1862, but his parents brought him to New Orleans in 1864.[12] Abraham Brittin, a native of Washington in Hempstead County, Arkansas, arrived in New Orleans when he was eleven years of age.[13] Dr. H. Dickson Bruns, another Citizens' League stalwart, was born in Charleston, South Car-

9. *The Citizens' League: A History of the Great Reform Movement in New Orleans, April 21, 1896* (New Orleans, n. d.), pp. 6, 18, 24, 74.
10. *Daily States*, December 19, 1896.
11. *The Citizens' League*, 4, 30, 48.
12. *The Citizens' League*, 18, 55, 62, 76.
13. *Who's Who in Louisiana and Mississippi* (New Orleans, 1918), p. 36.

olina, in 1859, but he came to New Orleans with his father, Dr. J. Dickson Bruns, after the Civil War.[14] John M. Parker, a native of Bethel Church, Mississippi, was nine years old when his family moved to New Orleans permanently in 1872.[15]

Few Citizens' Leaguers came to New Orleans from other sections of the United States and from abroad. Ten were born in the Northeast and seven were native to the Midwest. Only twenty-eight charter members were immigrants, all from western Europe. Fourteen were born in Ireland, six were native to Germany and five were from England. Two were native Frenchmen, and one was from Switzerland (See Table 2).

The reformers who were born in the North and in Europe, nonetheless, followed the migration pattern of the native southerners. Most came to New Orleans when they were children. W. E. Dodsworth, for instance, was born in Council Bluffs, Iowa; his family moved to the Crescent City when he was thirteen years old. Peter F. Gillen was born in New York in 1851, but he received his education in the Christian Brothers and public schools in New Orleans. William G. Turner, a native of Sauk City, Wisconsin, came to the city when he was only nine years old. A. G. Ricks, a native of Germany, was a mere lad when he came to the city. Herman Meader was born in Prussia in 1841, and came to the city at a very young age. Edward Finnegan was born in Ireland in the year 1843 and came to the Crescent City when he was three years old. Louis Guillaud was, however, an atypical charter member of the Citizens' League. Guillaud, a native of Lyons, France, came to this country when he was twenty years old.[16] He was one of the few reformers who moved to New Orleans in adulthood.

14. *Biographical and Historical Memoirs of Louisiana,* 2 vols. (Chicago, 1892), I, 324.
15. Matthew J. Schott, "John M. Parker of Louisiana and the Varieties of American Progressivism" (Ph.D. dissertation, Vanderbilt University, 1969), pp. 6-7.
16. *The Citizens' League,* pp. 28, 29, 44, 46, 48, 56, 70.

The majority of the mothers and fathers of American-born charter members of the Citizens' League were native to the United States (See Table 3). Forty-one of the fathers and sixty-one of the mothers were Louisiana-born. An additional forty-two of the fathers and forty-one of the mothers were native southerners.

Although most of the parents of the Citizens' Leaguers were native Americans, several were immigrants. Those immigrant parents, like the charter members, were mainly from western Europe. Twenty-nine fathers and thirty mothers were from Ireland, twenty-one fathers and fifteen mothers were born in Germany and sixteen fathers and eleven mothers were native to France (See Tables 4 and 5). Only three parents came from Martinique. One mother was born in Cuba; one father was a native of Santo Domingo. Several of the reformers were the children of one immigrant parent and one native-born parent. Jacob H. Abraham, for example, was the son of a German father and an Alabama-born mother.[17] Paul Capdevielle's father was French; his mother was a native Louisianian.[18] Robert E. Craig was the child of an Irish father and a Mississippi-born mother.[19]

Few charter members of the Citizens' League lived near the central core of the Crescent City. Only nineteen of the reformers (8.1 percent) resided within nine blocks of the corner of Canal and Royal Streets, the site of the Henry Clay statue and the primary meeting spot in downtown New Orleans (See Table 6). An additional fifty-eight Citizens' Leaguers (24.7 percent) lived within the next ten-block radius. The remainder, the great majority (67.2 percent), lived twenty or more blocks from the urban core. Four charter members (1.7 percent) lived across the Mississippi River in Algiers. E. L. Bemiss lived in adjacent St. Bernard Parish.[20]

17. Twelfth United States Census of Population, 1900, Louisiana, Volume 30, Orleans Parish, New Orleans City, Reel 575.
18. Ibid., Volume 26, Reel 572.
19. Ibid., Volume 28, Reel 574.
20. Soards, 1897, p. 110.

Most Citizens' Leaguers lived above Canal Street (See Table 7). This residential distribution, however, partially reflected the configuration of the city and the division of local wards. Ten city wards (wards 1, 2, 3, 10, 11, 12, 13, 14, 16 and 17) were located above Canal Street. Only six wards (wards 4, 5, 6, 7, 8 and 9) were downtown. Algiers formed a separate ward (ward 15).

Residential preferences were further evidenced by the number of reformers who lived in each municipal ward. The charter members of the Citizens' League made their homes primarily in the suburban neighborhoods of uptown New Orleans (See Table 8). One hundred thirty-five members of the reform organization (57.5 percent) lived in the Tenth, Eleventh, Twelfth, Thirteenth, Fourteenth, Sixteenth and Seventeenth Wards. These seven municipal wards encompassed the exclusive Garden District and other fashionable neighborhoods in the uptown section of New Orleans. Conversely, only one (0.4 percent) and three (1.3 percent) of the charter members lived in the Eighth and the Ninth Wards, respectively. These two city wards were the farthest away from Canal Street in the opposite direction.

Several members of the reform faction were neighbors. Forty-four Citizens' Leaguers (18.7 percent), for example, had residences in the Garden District, a wealthy, sixty-five-block area in uptown New Orleans.[21] Many of the reform stalwarts lived on the same street; several indeed resided on the same city block. Dr. H. Dickson Bruns, Walter D. Denegre, Horace Gumbel and George B. Penrose had homes in the 2300 block of Prytania Street.[22] Lucien N. Brunswig, William F. Pinckard and John S. Rainey lived three blocks up the street.[23] A total of nineteen charter members of the

21. *The WPA Guide to New Orleans*, p. 349. The boundaries of the Garden District were Magazine Street, Louisiana Avenue, Jackson Avenue and St. Charles Avenue.
22. *Soards, 1897*, pp. 159, 385, 681; Twelfth United States Census of Population, 1900, Volume 28, Reel 574.
23. *Soards, 1897*, p. 693; Twelfth United States Census of Population, 1900, Volume 29, Reel 574.

Citizens' League lived on Prytania Street. St. Charles Avenue was another popular place of residence among Crescent City reformers. Twenty-six charter members of the Citizens' League resided along the main thoroughfare of uptown New Orleans.[24] These men undoubtedly rode the St. Charles Avenue streetcar to and from work each day and probably shared their views on public affairs along the way.

The majority of the Citizens' League charter members were middle-aged and elderly men. Only seventy-eight members (33.2 percent) were forty years old or younger at the close of the nineteenth century (See Table 9). Most were older. Seventy-five of the charter members (32.3 percent) had been born during the decade of the 1850s. Fifty-four 23.3 percent) began life in the 1840s. Twenty members (8.6 percent) had been born in the decade of the 1830s. Five charter members of the Citizens' League had been born in the 1820s.[25]

The Citizens' League, to be sure, had a core of young vigorous members who would support the cause of good government for many years to come. John M. Parker, for instance, would endorse the Good Government League in 1912, later join the Progressive Party and in 1920 become the Democratic governor of Louisiana.[26] The advanced age of several Citizens' Leaguers, nonetheless, boded ill for the organization's future. Nine charter members did not live to witness the dawn of the twentieth century. John W. Labouisse, indeed, did not survive the official incorporation of the reform group; he died on December 7, 1896.[27] An additional twenty-five charter members were dead before 1906,

24. *Soards, 1897, passim.*
25. The five were Henry Bezou, Henry C. Boucher, Isaac E. Glenny, Louis Grunewald and Simon Toby. *Daily Picayune*, August 28, 1898, January 7, July 7, 1901, May 5, 1904; *Times-Picayune*, March 2, 1919.
26. Matthew J. Schott, "John Milliken Parker," in David C. Roller and Robert W. Twyman, ed., *The Encyclopedia of Southern History* (Baton Rouge, 1979), p. 955; *Times-Picayune*, May 21, 1939. See also Schott, "John M. Parker of Louisiana," *passim.*
27. *Daily Picayune*, December 8, 1896, February 3, August 29, 1897, January 1, August 28, 29, 1898; *Daily States*, December 13, 1897, August 21, 1898; *Times-Democrat*, February 3, 1897.

the ten-year anniversary of formal incorporation.[28]

The charter members of the Citizens' League represented the business and professional elite of the Crescent City. One hundred sixty-one of the good government backers were businessmen (See Table 10). Within their number were several of the most notable entrepreneurs in New Orleans. E. L. Bemiss, for example, was president of the Algiers Water Works and Electric Company and secretary-treasurer of the Edison Electric Company. Henry M. Preston, William J. Brophy, Nicholas Burke, Christopher Doyle, Henry Lochte, Albert Mackie and William J. Montgomery were grocers.[29] Jacob H. Abraham, Maurice Stern, Abraham Britten, John M. Parker and Horace Gumbel were among sixteen Citizens' Leaguers who were cotton brokers. Felix Couturie, one of the cotton brokers, was the president of the New Orleans Cotton Exchange.[30] Justin F. Denechaud owned the Denechaud Hotel. Paul J. Gelpi was a wholesale liquor dealer.[31] Paul Capdevielle, Charles Janvier, William Lyman and William H. Byrnes were presidents of insurance companies.[32] John A. Muir, Joseph Fromherz, Charles Garvey, William H. Krone and Ferdinand Reusch, Jr. were builders. Augustin B. Wheeler and George W. Young were bank presidents. Adolph G. Ricks, a leather goods merchant, was also vice-president of the Metropolitan Bank. Patrick Mc-Closkey, a commission merchant, was president of the New Orleans Board of Trade. John S. Rainey headed the New Orleans Chemical Company.[33]

28. *Daily Picayune*, March 21, April 5, August 12, October 12, December 1, 1900, January 7, July 7, 1901, July 23, November 3, 25, 1902, February 17, June 7, September 10, 1903, November 2, December 16, 1904, June 6, December 31, 1905; *Times-Democrat*, February 8, April 28, May 5, 6, June 17, August 28, September 6, 1904, April 22, 23, 1905.

29. *Soards, 1897*, pp. 110, 152, 273, 542, 572, 623, 703.

30. *Ibid.*, pp. 62, 150, 225, 363, 385, 407, 501, 534, 592, 673, 683, 693, 822; *The Citizens' League*, p. 4; *Times-Democrat*, December 8, 1896; *Daily States*, February 3, 1897.

31. *Soards, 1897*, p. 354; *Daily Picayune*, April 18, 1896.

32. *The Citizens' League*, p. 6; Kendall, *History of New Orleans*, II, 826-827; *Soards, 1897*, pp. 178, 552.

33. *Soards, 1897*, pp. 340, 349, 557, 634, 724, 730, 903, 930; *Times-Democrat*, April 28, 1904.

Several of the reform advocates had diversified commer-
cial interests. Paul Capdevielle, president of the Merchants
Insurance Company, for instance, was also president of the
Orleans Railroad Company and treasurer of the New Orleans Cold Storage Company. Isadore Hernsheim, vice-
president of S. Hernsheim and Company, Limited, a cigar
manufacturing firm, was additionally the president of the
National Automatic Fire Alarm Company of Louisiana, the
Crescent Hotel and News Company, the American District
Telegraph Company and the Southern Mineral Company,
vice-president of the Home Insurance Company and a director of the Whitney National Bank. Robert E. Craig was
the president of the New Orleans Water Works and vice-
president of the Sun Mutual Insurance Company and the
New Orleans National Bank. Robert M. Walmsley was
president of the Louisiana National Bank, the Southwest-
ern Building and Loan Association, the Orleans Traction
Company and the Crescent City Railroad Company.[34]

Business, not politics, was often the initial tie that united
many of the Citizens' League charter members. Charles
Janvier, Robert E. Craig and Fergus G. Lee, to cite several
key examples, were, respectively, the president, vice-president and secretary of the Sun Mutual Insurance Company.
J. Wallace Johnson was a branch manager. Benjamin F.
Eshleman and Walter R. Stauffer were partners in a successful hardware company. Joseph Fromherz and John A.
Muir owned a contracting firm. Emilien Perrin was a cotton
broker with A. Britton and Company. Joseph M. Rice and
James J. Clark were associates with Christopher Doyle in the
wholesale grocery business. Charles S. Judson and Frank D.
Mitchell were, respectively, a clerk and a salesman with Jo-
seph Bowling Company, Limited, B. Winchester Bowling's
firm. Frank Dameron was a clerk for Michael F. Dunn and
Company, stationers.[35]

    34.   The Citizens' League, p. 18; Soards, 1897, pp. 178, 226, 418, 884.
    35.   Soards, 1897, pp. 140, 202, 226, 237, 273, 282, 300, 321, 340, 358, 459,
468, 524, 617, 634, 683, 727, 820; The Citizens' League, p. 6.

Professional men formed the second largest occupational grouping among the charter members of the Citizens' League (See Table 10). Sixty-six good government supporters (28.1 percent) worked in the various professions. Most, forty-five, were lawyers and notaries. Eighteen were in the field of medicine. Twelve were physicians; six, pharmacists. Sidney Story, creator of "Storyville," the legalized redlight district in downtown New Orleans that, to Story's eternal chagrin, bore his name, and Simon Toby, editor of the New Orleans *Daily States*, were the only two journalists. George Soule, president of Soule's Commercial College and Literary Institute, was the sole educator among the charter members.[36]

Several of the physicians, however, merited inclusion in the category of educators because they held positions in the medical department of Tulane University. Dr. Stanford E. Chaille, for example, was dean of the medical school. Drs. Isadore Dyer, Charles Chassaignac, John B. Elliott, Erasmus D. Fenner and Paul Archinard were faculty members. They indeed constituted most of the institution's medical faculty. Dr. H. Dickson Bruns held a temporary post in the medical department as a lecturer on eye diseases.[37]

The professional ties that these doctors exhibited, like those of the businessmen, were also evident among the attorneys in the Citizens' League. George Denegre, Joseph P. Blair and Walter D. Denegre, for instance, were partners in the law firm of Denegre, Blair and Denegre. Hugh A. Bayne also worked for the firm. Charles P. Fenner and Samuel Henderson, Jr., were also law partners. So were William C. Dufour and George W. Moore. Some of the lawyers pursued commercial activities that connected them with other members of the Citizens' League. Richard H. Lea, to cite one

36. *Soards, 1897*, pp. 812, 852; *Daily Picayune*, April 17, 1896; *Times-Picayune*, July 17, 1937.
37. John Duffy, *The Tulane University Medical Center: One Hundred and Fifty Years of Medical Education* (Baton Rouge, 1984), pp. 61-69, 72, 75, 77, 104.

example, was also the assistant secretary of the New Orleans Cotton Exchange. Bernard McCloskey was another
attorney with extensive business associations. Paul Capdevielle and Walter C. Flower were attorneys who abandoned the practice of law for the excitement and profits of
the business world.[38]

Few Citizens' League charter members belonged to the
laboring classes. Seven (3.0 percent) were skilled crafts-
men. James W. Kelly was the only unskilled worker. He,
however, was hardly ordinary. Kelly, a cotton yardman,
became president of Cotton Yardmen's Benevolent Association as well as "one of the most prominent men in labor
circles." He later shifted his energies to politics and in 1896
won election to the office of recorder of mortgages on the
Citizens' League ticket.[39]

A sincere desire to improve the quality of municipal government in their hometown certainly motivated most New
Orleans reformers. However, some charter members of the
Citizens' League perhaps harbored less honorable reasons
for their political involvement. While the Regular Democrats were in power, the reform-oriented entrepreneurs who
owned businesses that could benefit from close ties with City
Hall had little chance at government contracts. These men,
however, undoubtedly perceived the commercial opportunities that could come their way if the reform forces seized
control of city government. The good government advocates included contractors, painters, lawyers, bankers and
stationers who conceivably stood to profit directly and in-
directly from the success of the Citizens' League at the polls
(See Appendix 1).[40]

The charter of the reform organization admittedly pro-
hibited its officers from holding government posts, but the

38. *Soards, 1897*, pp. 103, 124, 254, 279, 312, 414, 521, 624; *Times-Picayune*, August 14, 1922, May 23, 1942.
39. *The Citizens' League*, p. 66.
40. For a view of municipal reformers' motives, see Samuel P. Hays,
"The Politics of Reform in Municipal Government in the Progressive Era,"
*Pacific Northwest Quarterly*, LV (October 1964), pp. 157-169.

stunning victory of 1896, nonetheless, swept numerous Citizens' Leaguers into public positions. The mayor, comptroller, commissioner of public works and the commissioner of police and public buildings were charter members of the good government group. Five of the six recorders' court judges and all four city court judges were Citizens' Leaguers. So were the civil sheriff and his clerk, the criminal sheriff and his clerk, the recorder of mortgages, the register of conveyances, the coroner and the district attorney. Three of four city court clerks and two of four constables were charter members of the Citizens' League. Reformers also occupied twenty-three seats on the city council. An additional five charter members represented the Crescent City in the state senate. Seventeen served in the lower house.[41]

The presence of so many reformers in Crescent City government after 1896, however, belied a disquieting reality about those Citizens' Leaguers in public office. Most were political amateurs and several were outright novices. Mayor Walter C. Flower, to note the outstanding example, had "never occupied a public office before." Felix Couturie was another reform leader who "had never taken active part in political affairs until recently, when he joined the Citizens' League. . . ." Edward J. Thilborger also was a newcomer to the political wars. A Citizens' League publication stated: "This is the first time Mr. Thilborger held an office, in fact the first time he actively engaged in any political movement." Walker B. Spencer was still another reformer who "had never, prior to the campaign of last year [1896], taken any active part in politics." Orris I. McLellan was also a political neophyte. He had "never taken a very active part in politics until the recent election, when he was elected to the Legislature, where he is now serving." Grocer Herman Meader was one more reform leader who "while always exercising his right of franchise never participated actively in politics. . . ." Councilman J. Henry Lafaye had previously

41. *The Citizens' League,* pp. 40-42.

"never been engaged in politics, simply doing his duty as a citizen, preferring to let others reap the glory."[42]

Those Citizens' Leaguers with prior political experience were commonly veterans of the Young Men's Democratic Association, a reform faction that had successfully challenged the Regular Democrats in the municipal campaign of 1888. A surprisingly few of the Citizens' League charter members, however, were triumphant candidates in that electoral contest. Abraham Britton, Philip Hirsch and George L'Hote were the only three Citizens' Leaguers to win seats on the city council in 1888. Charles W. Drown became criminal sheriff. Dr. Yves R. LeMonnier was the coroner and Dr. Paul E. Archinard became his assistant. Richard H. Lea was judge of the Fifth Recorders' Court. Michael DeLucas was the clerk of the Fourth City Court of New Orleans. Robert M. Walmsley became president of the New Orleans Board of Debt Liquidation.[43] Felix J. Dreyfous and Frank Marquez were the only charter members of the Citizens' League to gain election to the state legislature in 1888.[44]

Most Citizens' Leaguers with previous political experience, however, apparently followed the example of William G. Turner, a councilman during the Flower administration. Turner had been "ever active in any movement looking to the betterment of the city and although a hard worker in the many reform movements set on foot he never accepted office until the present." Joseph F. Herberger, too,

42. *Ibid.*, pp. 4, 19, 26, 49, 52, 72.
43. *Soards, 1889*, pp. 1082-1083, 1085. Several Citizens' Leaguers also participated in the Anti-Lottery League, a good government group that in 1892 succeeded in the election of Governor Murphy J. Foster, an opponent to the gambling interests, but failed to prevent the victory of Mayor John Fitzpatrick of New Orleans, a Regular Democrat who backed the Louisiana Lottery Company for the sake of his party. For the involvement of charter members of the Citizens' League in the Anti-Lottery League, see the Justin F. Denechaud Papers, Louisiana Historical Center, Louisiana State Museum, Old U. S. Mint Building, New Orleans, Louisiana. See also Jackson, *New Orleans in the Gilded Age*, Chapter 5.
44. Louisiana Legislative Council, *Membership in the Legislature of Louisiana, 1880-1980* (Baton Rouge, 1979), p. 102.

"always interested himself in political reform movements, but never held any office before." Judge William R. Richardson of the First City Court of New Orleans also fit this mold. The judge, despite extensive political experience, particularly in the gubernatorial campaign of Francis T. Nicholls in 1876, nonetheless, was holding public office for the first time. Peter Clement, judge of the Fourth Recorders' Court in New Orleans, was another reformer who had "always taken an active part in politics, but until the late election never held a public office."[45]

For many Citizens' Leaguers, the public office that they held during the Flower administration marked their sole foray into political life. Councilman George M. Leahy was typical. At the time of his death in 1923, the New Orleans *Times-Picayune* stated: "His only political office was as a reform councilman during the Flower administration."[46] Leahy and many of his reform associates were political amateurs. Although several of the charter members of the Citizens' League were able politicos who understood the fine art of campaigning and the need for strong organization, they were essentially business and professional men who entered politics for the sake of principle. They did not depend upon politics for their livelihood, nor did they appreciate the nuances of neighborhood politics that served the Regular Democrats so well. The political naiveté of these reformers, like their age, was an undeniable liability to the cause of good government in New Orleans.[47]

Charter members of the Citizens' League displayed varied educational backgrounds. Most had attended college and many had continued their educations in graduate and professional schools (See Table 11). Several had attended excellent schools abroad. Dr. Yves R. LeMonnier graduated from the Medical School of Paris. Dr. Paul S. Reiss attended

45. *The Citizens' League*, pp. 30, 46, 49, 69.
46. *Times-Picayune*, November 1, 1923.
47. See Kenneth T. Jackson and Stanley K. Schultz, ed., *Cities in American History* (New York, 1972), pp. 369-370.

the University of Paris and completed his education in the medical department of Tulane University. T. Marshall Miller attended the University of Virginia Law School. Thomas Bayne went to Yale University. Robert B. Parker and William J. Montgomery attended Princeton University. John W. Labouisse was a Harvard man. William R. Lyman went to both Harvard and the University of Virginia. Joseph P. Blair and Leigh Carroll also attended the University of Virginia.[48]

Most of the doctors and lawyers who belonged to the Citizens' League were graduates of the medical and law departments of Tulane University. Many were classmates. Bernard McCloskey, Hugh C. Cage and Robert H. Marr, for example, graduated from the law department in 1882. Attorneys John St. Paul, Andrew Fitzpatrick and David B. H. Chaffe belonged to the class of 1886. Felix Puig, Frank E. Rainold, William C. McLeod and Patrick Hennessey were members of the law class of 1889. George Untereiner, J. Porter Parker and Thomas J. Duggan graduated from the Tulane law department in 1895.[49]

A significant number of Citizens' Leaguers (26.4 percent), however, did not progress beyond an elementary education. George W. Young, for instance, "was educated in the Catholic parochial schools and the public schools" in New Orleans. He "left school at the age of 14, at the death of his father." Charles W. Drown joined the Quartermaster Department of the Confederate Army at the age of thirteen. John A. Muir, the builder, attended "the public schools and then apprenticed himself to learn the carpenter trade, which he mastered when quite young." James J. Clark "was but 14 years old when he entered the house of Smith Bros & Co." William L. McGary was another Crescent City reformer who

48.  *Biographical and Historical Memoirs of Louisiana,* I, 295, 543, 551-552; *Times-Democrat,* December 8, 1896; *Daily Picayune,* December 20, 1908; *Times-Picayune,* November 7, 1918, September 1, November 26, 1920, October 27, 1927, September 13, 1932, August 21, 22, 1934, November 9, 1919.
    49.  *The Tulane News Bulletin,* II, (May 1922), p. 2; *ibid.,* p. 7 (December 1926), pp. 1-2; *ibid.,* p. 9 (April 1929), p. 1; *ibid.,* p. 10 (November 1929), pp. 1-2.

left the public schools for the business world. McGary was "a mere boy" when he "obtained employment with the big commercial firm of Woods, Matthews & Co., on Poydras street." For these men and other charter members of the Citizens' League, education gave way to enterprise at an early age.[50]

The success of the reformers' various commercial and professional endeavors was evident in the magnitude of their accumulated wealth. Among the members of the good government organization were some of the richest men in New Orleans. In 1897, nine members of the Citizens' League had real estate and personal property assessed at more than $100,000. Louis Grunewald, owner of a hotel and a lucrative music business, was the wealthiest reformer. His property had an assessed worth of more than $450,000. Commercial druggists Isaac L. Lyons and Lucien N. Brunswig held taxable wealth of $258,500 and $142,300, respectively. Benjamin Eshleman and Walter R. Stauffer, partners in a successful hardware company, possessed property holdings that exceeded $160,000 in assessed value. So did grocers Henry Lochte and Henry M. Preston. Nicholas Burke, another grocer, and Orris I. McLellan, head of the McLellan Dock Company, owned more than $100,000 in real estate and personal property. Other reformers were financially comfortable. Commission merchant Wesley E. Lawrence held property assessed at $84,300. Others owned substantial—though lesser—amounts of assessed property. In 1897, for instance, Ferdinand Reusch, Jr., the contractor, had property valued at $32,775. William H. Dwyer, a dealer in notions, owned property assessed at $42,200. Most charter members of the Citizens' League possessed property holdings that were greater than $5,000 in value (See Table 12).[51]

Crescent City reformers, like most New Orleanians, were mainly Catholics. Nearly forty percent of the good govern-

50. *The Citizens' League*, pp. 20, 28, 46, 56, 62.
51. City of New Orleans Real Estate Tax Ledgers, 1896-1897, Louisiana Division, New Orleans Public Library.

ment supporters, however, were Protestants (See Table 13).
This sizable Protestant contingent was unusual in predom-
inantly Catholic New Orleans and indicated a possible par-
allel with the largely Protestant reform groups that were active in other American cities during the late nineteenth
century. Charter members of the Citizens' League belonged to all of the primary Protestant creeds. Frederick
Adolph, for example, was one of many Episcopalians. Burris D. Wood was a Methodist, Abraham Britton was Presbyterian and Leonard Naef and Adolph G. Ricks were
members of the Evangelical Lutheran Church. George Soule
was Unitarian. Jacob H. Abraham and Horace Gumbel were
two of six Jewish members of the Citizens' League. The reform organization clearly welcomed men of all faiths.[52]

Family ties as well as religion, occupation and education
often bound together charter members of the Citizens'
League. Elmer E. Wood, for instance, was the son of Burris
D. Wood. Bernard, John and Hugh McCloskey were brothers. So were attorney Charles P. Fenner and Dr. Erasmus
D. Fenner. Attorneys Walter D. and George Denegre, too,
were brothers. George Denegre was the brother-in-law of
Thomas L. Bayne, an attorney who also had large real estate holdings. William J. Montgomery was the brother-in-
law of J. Porter Parker. Contractor Joseph Fromherz was the
brother-in-law of Ferdinand Reusch, Jr. Reusch, too, was a
builder.[53]

Combat against the Republican-controlled Metropolitan
Police at the Battle of Liberty Place in 1874 formed a common bond for several charter members of the Citizens'

52. *Daily Picayune*, July 23, 1902, October 1, 1907; *Times-Democrat*, February 8, 1904; *Times-Picayune*. February 22, 1922, August 1, 2, 1932, June 6,
1934; Kendall, *History of New Orleans*, II, 827-830; *Who's Who in Louisiana and
Mississippi*, p. 219. For the Protestant orientation of urban reform movements in the United States during the late nineteenth century, see Raymond A. Mohl, *The New City: Urban America in the Industrial Age, 1860-1920*
(Arlington Heights, 1985), p. 109.
53. *Daily Picayune*, July 23, 1902; *Times Picayune*, November 7, 1918, July
9, 1924, August 22, 23, 1927; May 25, 1930; August 21, 22, 1934.

League. The reformers, like the Regular Democrats, embraced the spirit of September 14, 1874, and with ample justification. Thirty charter reformers were veterans of the White League (See Table 14). Citizens' League leader Charles Janvier was the outstanding example. Janvier, "in 1874, when but 17 years of age, . . . was a member of the Roman Rifles, commanded by Captain Charles Roman, and bore his part manfully in the historic struggle which gave the state clean government." George W. Young "was attached to Captain Shropshire's Company on the 14th of September. . . ." Other reformers who had taken part in the Reconstruction conflict were Mayor Walter C. Flower, Paul Capdevielle, a future mayor, Judge Gabriel Fernandez, George Denegre, Judge Edward Finnegan and James G. Jenkins, a business executive. Michael DeLucas did not participate in the actual battle, but "in 1874," he had been "on duty at the Carrollton station as a member of the White League." Dr. H. Dickson Bruns, furthermore, was the son of Dr. J. Dickson Bruns, "one of the organizers of the White League" who had also "established the 'Democrat' [a New Orleans newspaper] to fight the Kellogg administration."[54]

This professed reverence for the Battle of Liberty Place, however, masked an aspect of the New Orleans reform movement that most Citizens' League strategists undoubtedly preferred to keep cloudy. Although the great majority of the good government advocates were avowed Democrats, many Citizens' Leaguers found political accord with the Republicans and the Populists and welcomed their support in the municipal campaign of 1896.[55] Edward J. Thilborger, clerk of the Criminal District Court of New Orleans and a charter member of the Citizens' League, highlighted this coalition of convenience. He was a lifelong Republican.[56]

54. *The Citizens' League*, pp. 6, 20, 76; *Biographical and Historical Sketches of Louisiana*, I, 324; *Daily Picayune*, April 15, 16, 18, 1896, June 6, 1905; *Times-Picayune*, May 25, 1930.
55. Jackson, *New Orleans in the Gilded Age*, pp. 312-316.
56. Kendall, *History of New Orleans*, III, 946-947.

The volunteer fire department, a political training school for the Regular Democrats, attracted few reformers. Only six charter members of the Citizens' League were volunteer firemen (See Table 14). Judge Richard H. Downing was the most notable volunteer fireman. He had been president of two volunteer fire companies. Michael DeLucas also had been "a member of the volunteer fire department of the 7th district, and was one of the bravest men who ever fought for the lives of human beings and the property of the citizens of that district." DeLucas was also active in the Firemen's Charitable Association of the Seventh District.[57]

Citizens' Leaguers, however, were great participants in local social clubs. Thirty-five (14.9 percent) were Masons and thirty-one (13.2 percent) belonged to the Elks. Most reformers, however, seemed to gravitate toward the more prestigious social organizations. Nearly one third of the charter members of the Citizens' League belonged to the Boston Club and to the Chess, Checkers and Whist Clubs, respectively. Forty-two Citizens' Leaguers (17.9 percent) were members of the exclusive Pickwick Club (See Table 14). Paul J. Gelpi, John F. Tobin and Bernard McCloskey were among the eleven Citizens' League charter members who belonged to all three fashionable social organizations.[58] Reformers were also conspicuous within the major Mardi Gras krewes. Burris D. Wood (1886), George Soule (1887) and Charles Janvier (1896) had been Rex, King of Carnival. Augustin B. Wheeler (1897), Walter D. Denegre (1899), Frank B. Hayne (1904) and Hugh McCloskey (1913) were destined to be future monarchs of the School of Design. Paul Capdevielle had been king of Comus, an even older organization.[59]

57. *The Citizens' League*, pp. 70, 76.
58. *Who's Who in Louisiana and Mississippi*, p. 166; *Membership Roster of New Orleans Club, 1899* (New Orleans, 1899), no pagination.
59. *Daily Picayune*, July 23, 1902; *Times-Picayune*, August 14, 1922, January 22, 1927, August 4, 1935, February 28, 1938; Alcée Fortier, *Louisiana*, 3 vols. (Madison, Wisconsin, 1914), III, 123-124; Kendall, *History of New Orleans*, II, 399-400.

The charter members of the Citizens' League possessed an abundance of assets. They had wealth, social position, education and outstanding lineage. They unquestionably represented the economic and social elite of the Crescent City.

There were, however, important liabilities that were inherent in the composition of the Citizens' League. The reformers were generally older than the Regular Democrats. The Citizens' Leaguers, furthermore, lived mainly in the fashionable neighborhoods of uptown New Orleans. This concentration hampered the development of the citywide ward and precinct organizations that made the professional politicians strong. The reformers lacked political experience. They were political amateurs who gave most of their time and energy to the pursuit of their business and professional careers. For them, government and politics were secondary concerns. These traits did not portend a bright future for the reform movement in New Orleans. The Citizens' League, like previous reform groups in the Crescent City, could not sustain the political intensity that was necesary for consistent success at the polls. By 1899, the reform body was a nearly defunct organization. Political power in New Orleans reverted to the younger, more diligent and better organized professional politicians.

GEORGE J. GLOVER
General Contractor

*(Louisiana State Museum, New Orleans)*

J. M. Batchelor          Martin Behrman

Charles F. Buck          E. B. Kruttschnitt

*(Photographs: Louisiana State Museum, New Orleans)*

Adolph Meyer                  Jonathan A. Muir

A. G. Ricks                   George Soule

*(Photographs: Louisiana State Museum, New Orleans)*

COLONEL JOHN P. SULLIVAN
Attorney At Law

*(Louisiana State Museum, New Orleans)*

NEW ORLEANS WARDS, MID-1880s

# IV

# Men of Stability and Influence: The Regular Democrats of New Orleans

George Washington Plunkitt of Tammany Hall, perhaps the foremost philosopher of American urban politics, once likened big-city machines to "fine old oaks" that "went on flourishing forever."[1] The New York millionaire, a skilled political manipulator who proudly boasted that he "seen his opportunities and he took 'em," was hardly an unbiased observer, but his analogy certainly had merit.[2] In the nation's maturing cities, powerful political organizations, like mighty oaks, depended heavily upon healthy roots. Without a network of smoothly running political units at the ward, precinct and sometimes block level, urban machines stood little chance at the polls. Guiding these lesser political organizations was a small army of professional politicians, the ward bosses and precinct captains whom reformers often decried. These nameless, faceless foot soldiers of the urban electoral wars, nonetheless, provided the essential personal link between the machines and their diverse constituents. They offered succor to immigrants and other less privileged city dwellers, sliced bureaucratic red tape for legitimate businessmen and abetted those entrepreneurs who pursued less reputable enterprises, mainly gambling and prostitution. On election day, the neighborhood leaders consistently got out the vote. To the diligent, usually unheralded efforts of these men, nationally acclaimed city bosses owed their success.[3]

1. Riordon, *Plunkitt of Tammany Hall*, p. 17.
2. *Ibid.*, pp. 3-6.
3. See, for example, David R. Goldfield and Blaine A. Brownell, *Urban*

Martin Behrman, acknowledged head of the Regular
Democrats, successor to John Fitzpatrick in New Orleans
politics and one of the foremost urban bosses in the United
States during the early twentieth century, appreciated the
untouted contributions of his district leaders. In his published memoirs, the Crescent City politican noted: ". . . my
experience indicates that a great deal of the best service the
public gets is from the men relatively little known to the
public. Their wards know them. Their following knows
them. Many businessmen know them. But because they do
work that does not strike the reporters as sensational, they
are not known to the general public." The New Orleans
leader deplored the view that a "ward boss" was "a lazy fellow who dresses well, drinks often, smokes big cigars and
. . . [usually] does not work." Although Behrman conceded that many political posts required little effort, he
maintained that "the man who holds one of them and limits
himself to the job does not become a real leader."[4]

Behrman's respect for neighborhood politicians reflected
both his acumen and his own apprenticeship at the lower
levels of New Orleans politics, but his contention that these
men were largely anonymous was ironic. In the South's
largest city, the members of the Regular Democratic Organization (RDO), a formidable urban political machine, were
readily identifiable. This high visibility derived from the
close intermingling of the Old Regulars' ward and precinct
structure with an officially chartered club that ostensibly
advanced social and philanthropic as well as political goals.
An early example of this phenomenon was the Crescent
Democratic Club, founded in 1891. For five years, this organization formally promoted Democratic interests in the

---

*America: From Downtown to No Town* (Boston, 1979), pp. 285-293; Howard
P. Chudacoff, *The Evolution of American Urban Society* (Englewood Cliffs,
1981 edition), pp. 141-149; Alexander B. Callow, Jr., *The City Boss in America* (New York, 1976), *passim*.
    4.   Kemp, ed., *Martin Behrman of New Orleans*, pp. 59-60. See also Rior-
don, *Plunkitt of Tammany Hall*, pp. 45-49.

city.[5] In November 1896, however, the club dissolved after the Citizens' League defeated the Regular Democrats at the polls and forced the political professionals to accept the need for reorganization. One month later, New Orleans politicians gathered in the chambers of their defunct club to establish "a new Democratic club," the better known, more durable Choctaw Club of Louisiana.[6] A Regular Democratic brochure would later recall: "The Choctaw Club was born from the Crescent Democratic Club, which was formed in 1891."[7]

Because the New Orleans machine and its officially chartered appendage were virtually interchangeable, membership rolls constituted a directory of politically prominent Democrats in the Crescent City. At the turn of the century, two rosters identified the members of the urban political organization. The first was the original charter itself. Ninety-two founding members affixed their signatures to the document that created the Choctaw Club. Eighty-four signees were New Orleanians and eight were nonresidents.[8] When Charles T. Madison, of Monroe, Louisiana, later moved to the Crescent City, this ratio shifted by one.[9] Many nonresident members of the Choctaw Club were extremely important figures in their respective parishes and interacted with the New Orleanians in state government, but they exerted little clout within the urban organization. Their presence, nonetheless, signified the firm political ties that the New Orleans machine maintained with Democrats

5. Charter of the Crescent Democratic Club, May 23, 1891, Recorder of Mortgages, Civil District Court Building, New Orleans, Louisiana; Reynolds, *Machine Politics in New Orleans*, p. 32; Jackson, *New Orleans in the Gilded Age*, p. 54; T. Harry Williams, *Huey Long* (New York, 1969), pp. 188-189.

6. *Daily States*, November 23, 1896; *Times-Democrat*, December 29, 30, 1896; *Daily Picayune*, December 30, 1896, January 2, 1897; Kemp, ed., *Martin Behrman of New Orleans*, p. 344; Williams, *Huey Long*, pp. 188-189. See also Chapter 2.

7. Souvenir Program, Choctaw Club of Louisiana, Choctaw Day, Pontchartrain Beach, September 3, 1932.

8. Charter of the Choctaw Club of Louisiana.

9. *Who's Who in Louisiana and Mississippi*, p. 158.

throughout the state from the end of Reconstruction to the rise of Huey Long.[10]

In May 1902, a second list of members appeared when *Club Life*, a journal devoted to "southern clubdom," published a special issue on the Choctaw Club. A five-page roster accompanied a brief history of the organization. The history contained photographs and biographical sketches of outstanding members. This second listing indicated that the Choctaw Club had, within five years, expanded to 422 members. Three hundred fifty-eight were residents of New Orleans, sixty-four lived outside the city.[11]

These two lists yielded the names of 407 identifiable resident members of the Choctaw Club (See Appendix 2).[12] These men, under the leadership of John Fitzpatrick and his able protégé Martin Behrman, comprised the nucleus of the strongest political machine in the South. From the end of the nineteenth century to the mayoral election of 1946, the Regular Democrats of New Orleans lost only one municipal election.[13]

10.    Reynolds, *Machine Politics in New Orleans*, p. 33; Williams, *Huey Long*, pp. 188-189; Taylor, *Louisiana: A Bicentennial History*, pp. 132-137; Allan P. Sindler, *Huey Long's Louisiana: State Politics, 1920-1952* (Baltimore, 1956), pp. 22-26; Jackson, *New Orleans in the Gilded Age*, pp. 28-37.
11.    "Choctaw Club," pp. 6-10, *passim*. Captain Bernard "Ben" Mitchell, a river pilot, and John Dymond, Sr., a major figure in the Louisiana sugar industry, were actually political leaders in nearby St. Bernard and Plaquemines, respectively, but both had residences in New Orleans. Kendall, *History of New Orleans*, II, 778-781; *ibid.*, III, 1017; *Soards, 1900*, pp. 294, 614.
12.    The 1902 membership list contained two names that defied identification, T. C. Artope and C. N. Bear. Neither of the two names appeared in New Orleans city directories of the period. Their absence suggests two possibilities: the names were misspelled or the two men were actually nonresident members with improper notations on the membership list. The names of other 1902 members exhibited several similar errors. Since no information was available on these two names, they have been omitted from the composite sample of Regular Democrats. "Choctaw Club," p. 6.
13.    See Edward F. Haas, *DeLesseps S. Morrison and the Image of Reform: New Orleans Politics, 1946-1961* (Baton Rouge, 1974), pp. 8-40. The sole defeat came in 1920 when Andrew J. McShane, a local businessman and reform candidate who had the backing of Governor John M. Parker, outpolled Martin Behrman. Kemp, ed., *Martin Behrman of New Orleans*, p. 314n.

The great majority of Old Regulars, a group devoted to the advancement of Democratic interests in the state, were fittingly native Louisianians (See Table 15). Many were born and raised in the Crescent City and often boasted a proud lineage. René LeGardeur, for instance, possessed a "family name" that, according to journalist and author John Smith Kendall, "has been one of honorable associations in New Orleans for several generations."[14] In May 1902, *Club Life* reported that Charles Janvier, one of twenty-seven ex-Citizens' Leaguers who joined the Choctaw Club, "is a native of New Orleans, and is a descendent of one of the oldest Creole families in this State." His ancestors first arrived in America from France in 1686.[15] Sidney Lewis, president of the Choctaw Club in 1901-1902, was the grandson of Judge Joshua Lewis, one of Thomas Jefferson's appointees to the Superior Court of the Territory of Orleans in 1807.[16] Mercer W. Patton was the son of I. W. Patton, a former mayor of New Orleans.[17]

Others who lacked distinguished ancestors, nevertheless, could claim birth and life-long residency in the Crescent City. Some, like Fernand Paletou, evidently strayed only rarely from their home neighborhoods. *Club Life* noted that Paletou was born February 13, 1873, in the Fifth Ward and continued to reside there.[18] Charles H. Brownlee of Algiers lived a similar existence.[19] Several Regular Democrats, like James Cullen and Thomas Connell of the Second Ward, were youthful pals who continued their friendship into adulthood and politics.[20]

Some machine politicos were born in the outlying parishes of Louisiana and later moved to New Orleans. These men commonly came to the Crescent City for their educa-

14. Kendall, *History of New Orleans*, III, 1095.
15. "Choctaw Club," p. 24; Fortier, *Louisiana*, III, 221.
16. Fortier, *Louisiana*, III, 256-259; "Choctaw Club," p. 11.
17. *Daily Picayune*, September 26, 1899.
18. "Choctaw Club," p. 30.
19. *Ibid.*, p. 26.
20. *Ibid.*, p. 14.

tion, often at Tulane University, and never returned home. The life of Hugh C. Cage, who was born on Woodlawn Plantation in Terrebonne Parish and studied law at Tulane University, illustrated this pattern. So, too, did the career of Alvin Edward Hébert, who was born on the family farm near Plaquemine, Louisiana, and matriculated in the Tulane law department.[21] Henry Garland Dupré, a native of Opelousas who also studied at Tulane University, received his law degree in 1896 and soon entered private practice in the Crescent City. He, too, followed this path to political success. Charles T. Madison, however, proceeded in a slightly different fashion. Although the native of Harrisonburg, like the others, studied law at Tulane University, he became city attorney of Monroe in 1892 and served in this position for four years before he returned to New Orleans to launch his private practice.[22]

Those Regular Democrats who were born outside Louisiana generally followed one of two paths to the Crescent City. Many were children, even infants, who came with their families to New Orleans. City strongmen John Fitzpatrick and Martin Behrman, to cite two notable examples, were natives of Burlington, Vermont, and New York City, respectively. Both were infants when their families moved to New Orleans. Remy Klock, another Regular stalwart, was born in Louisville, Kentucky, but he, too, at a young age moved with his family to the Crescent City. Many of Klock's closest friends did not realize that the politician was not native to New Orleans. John Dymond, Jr., another native of New York City, was eleven years old when his family moved south. C. Harrison Parker was twelve years old when he came to New Orleans.[23]

Those adults who relocated to the Crescent City usually pursued career interests. At age twenty-two, Edwin How-

21. Fortier, *Louisiana*, III, 81-82, 197.
22. *Who's Who in Louisiana and Mississippi*, pp. 76, 158.
23. *Item*, April 7, 8, 1919; *Daily States*, November 11, 1900, April 7, 1919; *Daily Picayune*, November 11, 1900; Fortier, *Louisiana*, III, 41, 720, 784.

ard McCaleb, a veteran of the Confederate Army, owning only $180.00 and four bales of cotton, "came to New Orleans friendless and unknown, sold his cotton for 54 cents a pound, realizing $1,360, and on this sum he supported himself while studying law in the office of . . . Judge Thomas Wharten Collens." On January 16, 1866, he was admitted to the Louisiana bar.[24] T. Marshall Miller, a former attorney general of Mississippi, resigned his post and in 1894 moved to New Orleans to enter a legal partnership with Eugene D. Saunders, whose previous law partner Edward Douglas White had accepted a seat on the United States Supreme Court.[25] Linus W. Brown, a native of Goshen, Orange County, New York, in 1879, at age twenty-three, "decided to seek fresh fields of labor, and with this end in view, accepted a position with the Southern Pacific railroad as mechanical engineer, with headquarters at New Orleans." Four years later, he opened his own engineering office.[26] The telegraph business prompted Robert Ewing to move from Mobile, Alabama, to the Crescent City.[27] J. R. Terhune, manager and state agent for the Western Union Telegraph Company in New Orleans, had previously been company manager in Lexington, Kentucky.[28] Most of the adults who relocated to New Orleans, unlike Linus Brown, were southerners who traveled only a short distance and undoubtedly considered the regional metropolis to be an alluring mecca (See Table 15).

Surprisingly few members of the Choctaw Club were immigrants. Although the political organization consciously sought and protected the immigrant vote, only fifty-six Choctaws at the turn of the century were foreigners.[29] Ireland and Germany contributed nearly one half of this total with fourteen and thirteen members, respectively. Those

---

24. *Biographical and Historical Memoirs of Louisiana*, II, 213-214.
25. Fortier, *Louisiana*, III, 783.
26. *Biographical and Historical Memoirs of Louisiana*, I, 321-322.
27. Kendall, *History of New Orleans*, II, 788.
28. "Choctaw Club," p. 50.
29. Cunningham, "The Italian," pp. 22-36. See also Chapter 2.

from England numbered six. France and Canada each contributed five. Italy was the birthplace of four Regular Democrats and two more were from Mexico. No other country
contributed more than one. The immigrant members of the
New Orleans machine, like many native Americans who
migrated to Louisiana from out of state, often came to the
United States with their families. Blayney T. Walshe, the first
vice-president of the Choctaw Club, for instance, was thirteen years old in 1853 when he came to the United States.[30]

The relatively small number of immigrant members,
however, was deceptive. Although few Regular Democrats
were foreign-born, the majority of the native American politicos were the children of aliens. Of the 334 native-born
Choctaws, 190 members (56.9 percent) had at least one foreign-born parent (See Table 16). The origins of the immigrant parents of native-born Regular Democrats closely followed the pattern of the immigrant members. Mothers and
fathers from Ireland, Germany and France, respectively,
predominated (See Tables 17 and 18). George Washington
Flynn with Irish parents, Martin Behrman with German
parents and Pierre A. Capdau with French parents were
typical. Others like Charles Bedell and Jules A. Grasser,
however, had mixed parentage. Bedell was the son of a
French father and a German mother; Grasser's father was
German and his mother was Irish.[31] They and their numerous political associates with foreign backgrounds indicated
clearly that the New Orleans Democratic machine was an
organization of immigrants and first-generation Americans.

Its members, unlike the Citizens' Leaguers, tended to live
near the center of the city. They, like the reformers, nonetheless, were often neighbors. One hundred seventy-three

30.   Twelfth United States Census of Population, 1900, Volume 31, Reel
575; "Choctaw Club," p. 1.
31.   Twelfth United States Census of Population, 1900, Volume 24, Reel
571; *ibid.*, Volume 27, Reel 573; *ibid.*, Volume 28, Reel 574; *ibid.*, Volume 31,
Reel 575.

Regular Democrats (43.1 percent) made their residence within nineteen blocks of the corner of Canal and Royal Streets, the heart of the city and the site of the Henry Clay statute (See Table 19). An additional 109 Choctaws (27.1 percent) lived within the next ten-block radius. Over seventy percent of all machine politicos in New Orleans therefore resided within twenty-nine blocks of the urban core. Only eleven (2.7 percent), conversely, lived seventy or more blocks from the Henry Clay statue. An additional seven (1.7 percent), including Martin Behrman, lived across the Mississippi River in Algiers.

Most Old Regulars, again like the members of the reform faction, made their homes above Canal Street, the city's main thoroughfare (See Table 20). The number of professional politicians who lived in each ward, however, affirmed their residential clustering near the city center. The Third Ward in the heart of town, the home district of municipal boss John Fitzpatrick, for instance, could boast fifty-six Regular Democrats in residence, the highest total for any city ward. The Sixteenth and Seventeenth Wards, the two municipal districts that were farthest uptown from Canal Street, on the other hand, could claim only five and three politicos, respectively. Twelve Regular Democrats lived in the Ninth Ward, the district farthest from Canal Street in the opposite direction. These three distant wards and Algiers could account for only 6.6 percent of all Choctaw Club members in the Crescent City (See Table 21).

Political professionals displayed another residential tendency that was irrespective of precinct, ward or distance from the city core; they, like the members of the Citizens' League, were often neighbors. In the Eleventh Ward, for example, Samuel J. Alston lived at 1005 Washington Avenue and William McLellan Fayssoux lived at Number 1006. Mark C. Sintes lived three blocks away at Number 1316. In downtown New Orleans, Mayor Paul Capdevielle lived at 2410 Esplanade Avenue and stockbroker Joseph T. Devereux made his residence at 2504 Esplanade. In the Garden

District, a neighborhood that also claimed several reform advocates, Charles G. Gill, Thomas M. Gill, Jr., Carston E. Torjuson, John Clegg, Frederick G. Ernst and Warren Easton lived along a five-block stretch of Third Street. Farther uptown, Hugh C. Cage and Charles Janvier, two former Citizens' Leaguers, had homes in the 1400 block of Webster Street. Henry G. Hester and Charles T. Madison lived at Number Six and Number Eleven Rosa Park, respectively.[32]

No neighborhood, however, could match the ten blocks along Canal Street between Claiborne Avenue and Broad Street for political representation. Within these ten blocks lived twelve Regular Democrats. An additional twenty-six politicians, furthermore, resided within two blocks of the main street in both directions. That John Fitzpatrick, the most powerful politician in the city, lived at 2024 Canal Street, the virtual center of this forty-block area, suggested the extent of his influence in the neighborhood. The New Orleans boss and his political neighbors constituted nearly ten percent of the entire Choctaw Club.[33]

Unlike its opposition, the New Orleans machine, with the energy of youth and the wisdom of maturity, was well equipped to meet the demands of urban politics. At the turn of the century, most Old Regulars combined both of the traits. Fitzpatrick and his faithful cronies John Brewster, Ferdinand Dudenhefer, Joseph Hirn and C. Taylor Gauche, all born before 1850, to be sure, remained effective leaders, but they were in a minority (See Appendix 2). So, too, were the young politicians who were born after 1870. In 1900, the

---

32.   *Ibid.*, Volume 26, Reel 572; *ibid.*, Volume 29, Reel 574; *ibid.*, Volume 29, Reel 575; *ibid.*, Volume 31, Reel 575.
33.   *Soards, 1900*, pp. 76, 85, 127, 202, 238, 327, 369, 574, 791, 828, 928. The twelve Regular Democrats were Thomas C. Anderson (2123 Canal), August M. Aucoin (2029 Canal), Peter A. Blaise (2104 Canal), Frank Chretien (2323 Canal), Charles Cuneo (2509 Canal), John Fitzpatrick (2024 Canal), Jeremiah M. and Walter L. Gleason (2638 Canal), Hugh McManus (1824 Canal), William E. Seebold, Jr., (2322 Canal), Clark Steen (2508 Canal) and Lawrence Wilt (2039 Canal). For the twenty-six nearby Regular Democrats, see Twelfth United States Census of Population, 1900, Volume 23, Reel 571; *ibid.*, Volume 24, Reel 571; *ibid.*, Volume 25, Reel 571.

majority of Regular Democrats were between the ages of thirty and fifty. One hundred twenty-two Old Regulars (30.7 percent) had been born during the 1850s. One hundred nineteen more (30.1 percent) had begun life during the following decade. Already asserting their political strength and yet aspiring to bigger triumphs, these men formed the core of the Regular Democratic Organization. Characteristic of this group was Martin Behrman, the ultimate successor to John Fitzpatrick. In 1900, the Algiers resident was thirty-six years old.[34] Because those Regular Democrats in their twenties numbered an additional seventy-two (18.1 percent), the future of the Crescent City machine looked bright. At the start of the twentieth century, 310 of its members (79.0 percent) were under fifty years of age (See Table 22).

George Washington Plunkitt and Martin Behrman frequently linked politics to business. The Tammany boss maintained that votes were "marketable goods" and advised young men that "the great business of your life must be politics if you want to succeed in it."[35] In his memoirs, Behrman contended that the "ability to get along with people and persuade them to vote with you is not much different from the ability to sell groceries and 'keep your trade,' as the saying goes."[36] This analogy was quite proper for the Regular Democrats of New Orleans since most of the Old Regulars, like their reform opponents, had occupational backgrounds in business. Two hundred forty-two members of the Choctaw Club of Louisiana (60.2 percent) first made their living in business (See Table 23). In 1900, John Fitzpatrick indeed informed his neighborhood representative of the United States Census Bureau that his occupation was "Capitalist" as did Old Regulars George W. Booth and Rudolph J. Goebel, two Crescent City businessmen who perhaps had more justification.[37]

34. *Who's Who in Louisiana and Mississippi*, p. 21.
35. Riordon, *Plunkitt of Tammany Hall*, pp. 9, 20.
36. Kemp, ed., *Martin Behrman of New Orleans*, p. 59.
37. Twelfth United States Census of Population, 1900, Volume 23, Reel 570; *ibid.*, Volume 23, Reel 571; *ibid.*, Volume 25, Reel 571.

Although several machine politicos including Martin Behrman, Bernard C. Sheilds and Adolph Meyer eventually abandoned the business world for the political arena, numerous members of the Choctaw Club, despite the admonitions of Behrman and Plunkitt, ably combined both activities.[38] In 1900, these men, more than the reformers, represented all levels of the New Orleans commercial community. Among them were some of the most prominent businessmen in the city. Charles H. Schenck, for example, was president of the Teutonia Bank, secretary-treasurer of the Standard Brewing Company, director of the Teutonia Insurance Company and the Teutonia Loan and Building Association and a leading member of the New Orleans Board of Trade.[39] John Bach, Joseph T. Devereux, Louis Maspero and Joseph A. Littlefield were stockbrokers. Henry Armbruster was president of the Standard Brewing Company and headed the Independent Oil Refining Company. Henry G. Hester was secretary and superintendent of the New Orleans Cotton Exchange. Louis Grunewald, the former Citizens' Leaguer, operated a thriving music firm, had a major interest in a hotel and was vice-president of Gardner Motors, Ltd.[40] Mayor Paul Capdevielle, Charles Janvier and Albert P. Noll were insurance executives.[41] Douglas M. Kilpatrick, president and treasurer of Jackson and Kilpatrick, Ltd., salt merchants, was president of the New Orleans Chamber of Commerce in 1900.[42] These men and the other entrepreneurs who allied with the Regular Democratic Organization prompted the machine's strong support

38. Harold Zink, *City Bosses in the United States: A Study of Twenty Municipal Bosses* (Durham, N. C., 1930); Kendall, *History of New Orleans*, III, 1028; *Memorial Addresses: Adolph Meyer* (Washington, D. C., 1909), p. 43, *passim*. For the views of Behrman and Plunkitt on businessmen in politics, see Reynolds, *Machine Politics in New Orleans*, p. 165; Riordon, *Plunkitt of Tammany Hall*, p. 20.
39. "Choctaw Club," p. 46.
40. *Soards, 1900*, pp. 81, 89, 426, 597, 826; *Times-Democrat*, June 1, 1900; *Times-Picayune*, March 2, 1915.
41. *Soards, 1900*, pp. 182, 459, 659.
42. *Times-Democrat*, June 4, 1905.

of the business community in the early twentieth century.[43]
For those local businessmen who relied heavily upon
government contracts, this political alliance was essential to
their financial success. Junius J. Garlick, for instance, was
the city bill poster.[44] George J. Glover, builder of "some of
the largest and most modern buildings in the City of New
Orleans" and "one of the best known general contractors in
the South with huge contracts, including several for the
Government of the United States," was a strong "believer
in the political doctrines represented by the Democratic
party. . . ." Frank J. Matthew, who "colored" the Crescent
City, "handled the largest painting contracts" in the region
for more than thirty years.[45] Julius D. Willis, Joseph Tran-
china, John L. Frawley and Fritz Jahncke were among eleven
additional contractors who belonged to the Choctaw Club
of Louisiana. Frank P. Mullen managed the Barber Asphalt
Paving Company. Peter J. O'Reilly manufactured elevators.
Conrad B. "Cooney" Fisher and William Markham Rhodus
were in the lumber business. Charles W. Corson, Joseph J.
Hooper, Thomas J. Moran and Bartholomew P. "Bat" Sullivan were stationers.[46] Victor Mauberret and Edward A.
Brandao were originally printers who later gravitated into
government service.[47]
During an era when saloons were important political
meeting places and Sunday-closing laws spurred serious
controversy, tavern keepers, liquor dealers and brewers
played an understandably prominent role in the Choctaw
Club. The most famous saloon proprietor among the Old
Regulars was Henry C. Ramos. In 1900, however, the creator of the renowned Ramos Gin Fizz was only one of twelve
bartenders in the political organization (See Appendix 2).

43. Reynolds, *Machine Politics in New Orleans*, pp. 138-140.
44. *New Orleans, Louisiana: The Crescent City* (New Orleans, 1903-1904),
p. 73.
45. *Who's Who in Louisiana and Mississippi*, pp. 101, 163. See also Fortier,
*Louisiana*, III, 178-180.
46. *Soards, 1900*, pp. 226, 325, 342, 438, 457, 632, 639, 731, 838, 863, 925.
47. *Times-Picayune*, October 8, 1918. See also Chapter 2.

Daniel A. Mayer, the former secretary of the Crescent Democratic Club, was a distiller's agent. Four more Choctaws were associated with breweries.[48]

Those Regular Democrats who engaged in enterprises that skirted the law absolutely required political connections. Thomas C. Anderson, president of the Record Oil Company, for instance, had financial interests in local houses of prostitution, established an intimate friendship with Josie Arlington, a notorious madam, and earned the nickname, the "Mayor of Storyville," a reference to his overt involvement in the city's legalized red-light district. An article in *Collier's* stated that "Anderson overtops the restricted district; he is its lawgiver and its king; one of the names for it is 'Anderson County.'" The pandering politico, nonetheless, was on a first-name basis with Martin Behrman and lived within hailing distance of John Fitzpatrick's home on Canal Street.[49] Martial H. "Marsh" Redon served another masculine vice. He was a bookmaker.[50] These men, of course, needed political protection to operate.

At the turn of the century, business as well as political ties linked members of the Choctaw Club of Louisiana. Charles H. Schenck's entrepreneurial activities clearly illustrated this pattern. Schenck and Henry Armbruster were officers of the Standard Brewing Company and Schenck and Albert P. Noll were associates in the Teutonia Insurance Company of New Orleans. Henry A. Veters sold hats for William Reinerth and Company.[51] In 1902, James F. Cannon was an agent for the Sun Life Insurance Company, Charles Janvier's firm.[52]

Professional men were also prominent in the ranks of the Crescent City political machine. One hundred nineteen

48. *Times-Democrat*, March 2, 1914; *Times-Picayune*, September 19, 1920. See also Chapter 2.
49. Al Rose, *Storyville, New Orleans* (University, Alabama, 1974), pp. 42-47. See also note 37.
50. *Soards, 1908*, p. 878.
51. "Choctaw Club," p. 46; *Times-Democrat*, December 24, 1909; *Times-Picayune*, October 24, 1917; *Soards, 1900*, p. 879.
52. *Soards, 1902*, p. 174.

lawyers and notaries, medical practitioners, engineers, educators and journalists (29.6 percent) comprised the Regular Democrats' second largest occupational contingent. Attorneys who commonly interacted with government and often sought political careers predictably constituted the most numerous subgroup (See Table 23). The benefits of political associations to New Orleans lawyers were frequently quite obvious. Joseph E. Generelly, to note a specific case, was the attorney for the local board of health.[53] Among the lawyers, professional and political relationships typically overlapped. Lamar C. Quintero, consul general for Costa Rica and legal advisor to the United Fruit Company, for instance, was the law partner of fellow Choctaw John Clegg, an ex-judge.[54] Other Regular Democrats who were also law partners included George F. Bartley and Carl C. Friedrichs, Charles F. Buck and George C. Walshe, Percy S. Benedict and Bernard McCloskey as well as Hugh C. Cage and Pierre Crabites. Attorney Jules A. Grasser, furthermore, worked with the law firm of McCloskey and Benedict.[55]

Relatively few men from laboring backgrounds joined the Choctaw Club of Louisiana during its formative period. Although the New Orleans machine openly championed the cause of workingmen after Reconstruction, only thirty-three skilled laborers (8.2 percent) and eight unskilled workers (2.0 perent) were active Old Regulars in the early twentieth century (See Table 23). Several workers, nonetheless, became outstanding politicos. One of the most successful was John Fitzpatrick, a carpenter by trade. Another was Peter Farrell, a warehouseman and later a cooper who served on the Democratic State Central Committee in 1900.[56]

Despite the diversity of occupational experiences among

53. Fortier, *Louisiana*, III, 177.
54. *Ibid.*, p. 805; "Choctaw Club," p. 38; *Times-Picayune*, October 31, 1921.
55. *Soards, 1902*, pp. 100, 111, 159, 169, 368.
56. *Item*, January 25, 1900; *Soards, 1880*, p. 297; *Soards, 1887*, p. 331. See also Chapter 2.

the machine stalwarts, the primary vocation of most Old
Regulars, unlike the reformers, was politics. In 1902, the year
when *Club Life* published its special issue on the Choctaw
Club, 203 Regular Democrats manned elective and appoin-
tive posts at all governmental levels. Congressman Adolph
Meyer and Robert C. Davey, the two representatives from
Orleans Parish, were the top federal officeholders. Charles
P. McEnery, son of the former governor and state supreme
court justice, was the assistant postmaster in New Orleans.
Secretary of State John T. Michel, Democratic leader in the
Thirteenth Ward of New Orleans; Superintendent of Edu-
cation Joseph V. Calhoun; and Louisiana Supreme Court
Justice Frank Adair Monroe were the highest ranking state
officials.[57] C. Harrison Parker, a former editor of the New
Orleans *Daily Picayune* and campaign manager for Francis
T. Nicholls and Murphy J. Foster, a man who had "ren-
dered incalculable service to his party," headed the Louisiana Board of Control, the agency that operated the state
penal system.[58]

The number of Old Regulars who held state jobs in Orleans Parish clearly evinced the strong bond between the
Crescent City machine and the Democratic administration
in Baton Rouge. Five of the seven state tax collectors in New
Orleans, including John Fitzpatrick and John Brewster,
leader of the Sixth Ward, belonged to the Choctaw Club.
Jeremiah Gleason was the registrar of voters. Robert Legier
was the recorder of mortgages and Emile Leonard was his
chief deputy. Anthony Sambola headed the conveyance office. Peter Farrell and Victor Mauberret, Old Regular leader
of the Fourth Ward, were state inspectors and gaugers of coal

57.　*Soards, 1902,* p. 1065; *Times Democrat,* March 9, December 27, 1908.
Lieutenant Governor Albert Estopinal, Auditor of Public Accounts W. S.
Frazee, State Treasurer Ledoux E. Smith, Attorney-General Walter Guion
and Justice Newton G. Blanchard were nonresident members of the Choctaw Club of Louisiana. "Choctaw Club," pp. 6-10. See also *Municipal Manual of the City of New Orleans, 1903* (New Orleans, 1903), *passim.*
58.　Quoted in Mark T. Carleton, *Politics and Punishment: A History of the
Louisiana State Penal System* (Baton Rouge, 1971), p. 37n.

and coke in Orleans Parish. Frank Zengal was public administrator for the state. William A. Kernaghan was secretary of the Port of New Orleans Board of Commissioners.
Clark Steen was the assistant secretary and treasurer. Edward L. Cope was the port superintendent.[59]
    Old Regulars also abounded in various sections of the state
judicial department in Orleans Parish. Thomas McC. Hyman was the clerk of the state supreme court. Thomas W.
Connell was clerk of the Orleans Parish Civil District Court
and Frederick D. King, John St. Paul, Walter B. Sommerville and George H. Theard were judges in four of its five
divisions. Joseph Garidel was minute clerk in Division C.
Isaiah D. Moore sat on the court of appeal and Charles H.
Brownlee was its clerk. Joshua G. Baker and Frank D. Chretien were the two criminal district court judges for Orleans
Parish. James A. Malloy, leader of the Eleventh Ward, was
the clerk. Arthur J. Desmond was minute clerk and Sturges
Q. Adams was stenographer for Section B of this court.
Henry Mooney was an assistant district attorney. John R.
Todd and Edward S. Maunsell were jury commissioners.[60]
    The Orleans delegation to the Louisiana General Assem-
bly also included several members of the Choctaw Club.
Hugh C. Cage was president pro tem of the state senate.
Among his colleagues were the Ninth Ward boss Ferdinand
Dudenhefer, George W. Flynn and Orris I. McLellan, a for-
mer member of the Citizens' League. Old Regulars, too, sat
in the state house of representatives. Legislators H. Garland Dupré, William McL. Fayssoux, Carl C. Friedrichs and
James C. Henriques were young lawyers on the rise, but the
most infamous representative was Thomas C. Anderson, the
"Mayor of Storyville." Robert S. Landry, furthermore, was
clerk-at-house and Thomas J. Ryan was the sergeant-at-
arms.[61]

59.  *Soards, 1902*, p. 1066.
60.  *Ibid.*, p. 1065.
61.  Official Roll of General Assembly of the State of Louisiana, 1900,
Louisiana Collection, Howard-Tilton Memorial Library, Tulane University, New Orleans, Louisiana.

The Old Regulars predictably dominated City Hall. Mayor Capdevielle and his chief clerk, the city treasurer, the city comptroller and his clerk, the commissioner of public works and his chief clerk, everyone in the city engineer's office, City Attorney Samuel L. Gilmore and four of his assistants, the commissioner of police and public buildings and his head clerk, the city notary, the custodian of notarial records and the entire board of assessors belonged to the Choctaw Club. Regular Democrats served in various capacities on all municipal boards. John J. Fowler, for example, was secretary and John J. Darrieux was assistant secretary to the New Orleans Board of Civil Service Commissioners. Dr. Mentor V. Richard was the coroner and Dr. S. Fitzhugh Mioton was his assistant. A. J. Parody was their clerk. P. Henry Lanauze was the recorder of births, deaths and marriages. William Mehle was president and James McRacken was president pro tem of the New Orleans City Council. Michael E. Culligan was the sergeant-at-arms.[62]

Regular Democrats were equally evident in the municipal court system. Members of the Choctaw Club were judges in the First and Second Criminal Courts of New Orleans, the First and Second City Courts and three of the five Recorders' Courts. In the First City Court of New Orleans, Louis Brehm was chief clerk, Charles R. Kennedy was constable and George W. Prados was chief deputy constable. Henry B. McMurray, leader of the Twelfth Ward, was the civil sheriff and Terence Reilly was the criminal sheriff.[63]

Professional politicians indeed were interlaced throughout municipal government in the Crescent City. James W. Kelly was the supervisor of streets for the upper district of the city. Meyer Dreifus was a clerk at the city prison. George W. Vandervort was secretary and property clerk for the New Orleans police force. William McCue was a clerk in the municipal tax mortgage office.[64]

62.   *Soards, 1902*, pp. 1058-1068.
63.   *Ibid.*, pp. 1064-1065.
64.   *Ibid.*, pp. 268, 543, 1058-1059.

The Regular Democrats, unlike the New Orleans reformers, moreover, were veterans of the political wars. Congressman Robert C. Davey, for example, had previously served three terms on the First Recorders' Court of New Orleans and three terms in the state senate. In 1888, he had been an unsuccessful candidate for mayor. Ferdinand Dudenhefer had served four terms in the state house of representatives and four years as a deputy in the city conveyance office before he moved into the tax office for the Third District. John Fitzpatrick had been a member of the state legislature, municipal administrator of improvements, commissioner of public works, mayor and a delegate to the state constitutional convention of 1898 before he became state tax collector in New Orleans. Henry B. McMurray had served two terms as clerk of the First City Court of New Orleans and two more on the local board of assessors before he won election to the post of civil sheriff. Blayney T. Walshe had been the administrator of finance in New Orleans, city treasurer and a member of the city council before he, too, became a state tax collector. These men and their colleagues were hardly political neophytes.[65]

For most Old Regulars, particularly the immigrants and the first-generation Americans, politics provided a means for upward mobility. Not all members of the New Orleans Democratic machine rose from the carpentry shop and the grocery story to the office of mayor as John Fitzpatrick and Martin Behrman, respectively, did or from the state legislature to the United States Congress as did H. Garland Dupré, but many achieved significant personal advancement.[66] William McCue, a bartender in 1900, was a municipal clerk two years later. Dairy farmer Baptiste Melun became a clerk in the city mortgage office. Vital Tujague,

65. "Choctaw Club," pp. 36, 48; *Daily States*, June 19, 1906, April 7, 1919; *Times-Democrat*, December 27, 1908; *Times-Picayune*, May 19, 1914, February 4, 1919; *Item*, April 7, 1919.

66. Fortier, *Louisiana*, III, 41; *Who's Who in Louisiana and Mississippi*, p. 76. See also Chapter 2.

another bartender, became city comptroller. Henry Puderer, a butcher in 1889, became assessor for the Sixth Municipal District. Joseph Hirn, a barber and captain of the Eighth Ward, also became an assessor.[67]

Educational levels as well as occupational backgrounds revealed that many of the Old Regulars were men who had come up the hard way. Several (22.2 percent) never advanced beyond elementary school (See Table 24). Joseph Hirn, John Fitzpatrick, Thomas C. Anderson, Jeremiah M. Gleason and numerous others attended only the New Orleans "common schools".[68] Martin Behrman, though a good student, quit school at age twelve when his mother died. John T. Michel, at age twelve worked as "office boy" in a lawyer's office. Both youngsters continued studying in their spare time. Robert Ewing attended private schools in his native city of Mobile until at age twelve he became a "messenger boy" in the telegraph office. George J. Glover remained in school until he was fourteen years old. Due mainly to his father's death, he quit school to help the family earn a living. "The meagre [sic] schooling of his earlier years" was "largely supplemented in the rigorous school of experience, the most successful of all teachers. . . ."[69]

Numerous members of the Choctaw Club, however, had extensive formal educations that included college and postgraduate study. Charles G. Gill, for instance, held a doctorate and a law degree from Tulane University. Several Old Regulars, moreover, attended fine schools outside Louisiana. Sidney Lewis earned his degree in civil engineering from the University of Virginia. Engineer William C. Kirk-

67.   *Soards, 1902*, pp. 268, 583, 1058. See also *Soards, 1889*, p. 724; *Soards, 1892*, p. 793.

68.   *Times-Democrat*, October 10, 1909; *Times-Picayune*, December 11, 1931; Democratic Party, Louisiana Central Committee, *The Convention of '98: A Complete Work on the Greatest Event in Louisiana's History, Together with a Historical Review of the Conventions of the Past and the General Assembly Which Called the Constitutional Convention* (New Orleans, 1898), pp. 38-40.

69.   Kendall, *History of New Orleans*, II, 188; *ibid.*, III, 942; Fortier, *Louisiana*, III, 41, 179; Zink, *City Bosses*, pp. 317-318.

land, a native Canadian, attended the School of Practical Science at Toronto University. E. Howard McCaleb, Jr., attended the University of Virginia and Harvard University before he was graduated from the law department at Tulane University. Henry Chiapella attended the University of Paris and Harvard University Law School as well as Tulane University.[70]

Since many of the lawyers and doctors who belonged to the Regular Democratic Organization were graduates of the law and medical departments of Tulane University, these professional men most likely met their future political cohorts for the first time in class. Percy S. Benedict, John Dymond, Jr., George W. Flynn, William L. Hughes and Lamar C. Quintero, for example, all were graduated from the Tulane law program in 1890. Nine future Old Regulars were members of the class of 1895. George Bartley and Carl C. Friedrichs, who later became law partners, completed their legal studies at Tulane University in 1898. So, too, did John P. Sullivan and Henry Mooney.[71]

The wealth of many Regular Democrats reflected their entrepreneurial and professional accomplishments. Among the richest Choctaws, however, were two former members of the Citizens' League who had defected to the New Orleans machine. In 1902, Louis Grunewald, one of the ex-reformers, with real estate and personal property assessed at $257,450, was one of the wealthiest men in the city. State Senator Orris I. McLellan, president of the McLellan Dock Company, the second one-time good government advocate, in 1901 held property valued at $100,250. Other Regular Democrats were merely well to do. Charles Wirth, a prominent commercial grocer, amassed property worth $66,880. Attorney Charles F. Buck, the unsuccessful Regular Democratic candidate for mayor in 1896, owned real es-

---

70. *Daily States*, January 23, 1898; *Times-Democrat*, March 10, 1911; *Times-Picayune*, July 29, 1933, November 1, 1945; "Choctaw Club," p. 50; *Tulane News Bulletin*, II (November 1921), pp. 25-26.

71. *Ibid.; ibid.*, 2 (May 1922): 151-152; *ibid.*, 3 (January 1923), p. 61.

tate assessed at $65,800. Brewer Peter A. Blaise and sugar entrepreneur Adam Gambell owned property valued at over $50,000. John Fitzpatrick, Henry C. Ramos, contractor Fritz Jahncke and attorney Pierre Crabites, though only twenty-four years old in 1902, were among the Old Regulars with real estate assessed at more than $25,000 (See Appendix 2).[72] The greatest number of Regular Democrats with recorded wealth in 1902, however, owned property that was valued at less than $5,000 (See Table 25).

These figures on the wealth of the Old Regulars, however, probably were misleading. Because the municipal tax ledgers listed only the assessed value of real estate and occasionally property on the premises, there was no record of income, stocks, bonds and bank accounts. The attachment of property to corporations also obscured true ownership. Regular Democrats, furthermore, often placed property in the names of their wives. Mayor Capdevielle, for example, held no property, but in 1902 Mrs. Capdevielle owned property valued at $16,000.[73] Controlling the real estate tax rolls was a significant advantage to the Old Regulars. The Crescent City machine also controlled the entire board of assessors.[74] In 1897, Louis Grunewald, then a member of the Citizens' League held property assessed at more than $450,000; five years later, the hotel and music company owner, now a loyal supporter of the Democrat machine, possessed property assessed at only $257,450. The seven Old Regular assessors quite likely gave preferential treatment to their political associates.

Most Regular Democrats were Catholics, but their religious preference was hardly surprising in a community with a predominant French heritage (See Table 26). Religion, however, apparently did not interfere in local politics. The Old Regulars included representatives of all major Protes-

72. City of New Orleans Real Estate Tax Ledgers, 1900-1902, Louisiana Division, New Orleans Public Library.
73. *Ibid.*
74. *Soards, 1902,* p. 1058.

tant denominations. John R. Todd, for instance, was a Baptist, William O. Hart was Presbyterian and Theodore H. Lyons was Unitarian. Assessor Henry Puderer attended Salem Evangelical Lutheran Church.[75] Congressman Adolph Meyer, Judge Isaiah Moore and Henry L. Lazarus, a leading attorney, moreover, were Jewish. Martin Behrman was the child of a Jewish family, but in later life he became a practicing Catholic and rented a pew at Holy Name of Mary Roman Catholic Church.[76]

Religion, residence, occupation and education tied together members of the Regular Democratic Organization, but numerous Crescent City politicians exhibited far stronger filial bonds. Victor Mauberret, a state coal gauger, was the father of Leon C. Mauberret, chief clerk in the city engineer's office, and the brother of Gustav Mauberret, a building permits clerk in the same municipal department. George C. Walshe was the son of political veteran Blayney T. Walshe and the son-in-law of Charles F. Buck. Stevedore Henry Peters was the father of attorney Theodore Peters. New Orleanian John Dymond, Jr., was the son of John Dymond, Sr., a nonresident member of the Choctaw Club and a leading figure in the Louisiana sugar industry who, though he had a residence in the Crescent City, represented the Fourth District in the state senate and played a major role in Plaquemines Parish politics. Young Dymond was also the son-in-law of Joseph Shakspeare, a former New Orleans mayor.[77]

Other family relationships were evident within the Crescent City machine. Dr. Charles Brunning and Henry J. Brunning, an attorney, were brothers. So were Baptiste Melun and Maurice Picheloup, despite their different surnames. John R. D. King, Jr., an appraiser in Division B, Civil

75. *Times-Picayune*, August 14, 1914, August 27, 1926, April 23, 1928, October 22, 1929.

76. *Daily Picayune*, March 9, 1908; *The Israelites of Louisiana* (New Orleans, n. d.) p. 79; Zink, *City Bosses*, pp. 317, 331.

77. "Choctaw Club," pp. 42, 54; Kendall, *History of New Orleans*, II, 778-781; *Times-Democrat*, July 3, 4, 1914; *Times-Picayune*, November 18, 1915.

District Court, was the nephew of Frederick D. King, the judge in Division D.[78]

For many Old Regulars, marriage established the familial connection. John P. Sullivan, for example, was John Fitzpatrick's son-in-law. Gus P. Cantrelle married the daughter of Alfred S. LeClerc. Attorney Walter L. Gleason and notary Robert Legier were brothers-in-law.[79]

Among several of the older members of the Choctaw Club, there was the common heritage of bravery in combat against the Republican-controlled Metropolitan Police of Reconstruction days. Twenty-five Old Regulars had fought with the Crescent City White League in the Battle of Liberty Place on September 14, 1874 (See Table 27). For these staunch supporters of Regular Democracy, participation in this struggle proved to be a valuable political asset for years to come. Clerk Thomas McC. Hyman, furthermore, achieved notoriety for protecting the records of the state supreme court during the battle. In his memoirs, Martin Behrman commented that, although he was only nine years old in September 1874 and certainly not a combatant, he had been on the scene and claimed a discarded Winchester rifle from the fray. Police Superintendent Dexter S. Gaster was another Choctaw who had not fought in the Battle of Liberty Place. Gaster, at the time a Metropolitan Police officer, had refused to fight the White League and thus won the acclaim of local Democrats. Although New Orleans reformers also boasted their share of participants in the Battle of Liberty Place, the ideal Democratic candidate for public office in the late nineteenth century was a distinguished veteran of the Reconstruction struggle against the Republicans.[80]

78. "Choctaw Club," p. 58; *Times-Picayune*, March 13, 1938; September 1, 1950.

79. "Choctaw Club," p. 52; *Who's Who in Louisiana and Mississippi*, p. 246; *Times-Picayune*, April 8, 1948.

80. Jackson, *New Orleans in the Gilded Age*, pp. 30-31; Kemp, ed., *Martin Behrman of New Orleans*, p. 246; *Daily Picayune*, August 14, 1901, June 29, 1909.

Participation in the city's volunteer fire department also had political implications. Because volunteer fire companies, like saloons, were political hotbeds during the Gilded Age, many ambitious young men received introductory political instruction and discussed the possibilities of public office during their long watches in Crescent City engine houses. Martin Behrman, for instance, belonged to the Algiers fire company; for many years, he was its treasurer. John Fitzpatrick and Remy Klock, long-time friends, were volunteer firemen in the Third Ward. Ring politicos Victor Mauberret and Thomas J. Ford were members of the Orleans Steam Fire Engine Company No. 21. Mauberret was its president. John Dahmer was the last volunteer chief of the Seventh District Fire Department in the Carrollton section of New Orleans. When the citizen firefighters gave way to professionalization and modernization, the former volunteers remained united through the Firemen's Charitable and Benevolent Association, an organization with clear political undertones. In 1881, Democratic Governor Louis Wiltz, a New Orleanian, was the association's vice-president. In 1902, John Fitzpatrick was president of the organization and Fifth Ward Councilman James McRacken, a Choctaw stalwart, was its secretary-treasurer.[81]

The camaraderie and political connections that the Regular Democrats cultivated in the volunteer fire companies were equally apparent in local social organizations. New Orleans politicos were expedient joiners. Fitzpatrick, for example, belonged to the Elks, Knights of Columbus, Ancient Order of Hibernians, Continental Guards, United Irish League of New Orleans and Irish Rifles of the Louisiana State Militia as well as the Fireman's Charitable and Benevolent Association and the Choctaw Club of Louisiana. He was also

81. *Daily Picayune*, April 14, 1896; *Item*, April 17, 1919; Thomas O'Connor, *History of the Fire Department of New Orleans* (New Orleans, 1895), p. 145; Zink, *City Bosses*, p. 319; *Soards, 1902*, p. 1098; Jackson, *New Orleans in the Gilded Age*, pp. 101-106.

a faithful contributor to the St. Mary's Orphan Asylum, his favorite charity.[82] Martin Behrman, however, surpassed his mentor. He belonged to the Merchants' and Manufacturers' Bureau, Elks, Press Club, Knights of Columbus, Benevolent Knights of America, German Benevolent Association, Ancient Order of Druids, Young Men's Social and Benevolent Association, Southern Yacht Club, Young Men's Gymnastic Club, Rotary Club and Chess, Checkers and Whist Club. He was also a trustee of Tulane University, the New Orleans Public Library and Delgado Trade School.

For Fitzpatrick and Behrman, membership in these various organizations was politically motivated. Behrman argued that a political leader must "see a lot of men. And often a lot of women besides." Clubs provided ample opportunity for these vital contacts. Although the Algiers politician stated emphatically that a successful ward boss must always exhibit the ability to "do things and get them done," he also noted the importance of "joining clubs and commercial organizations" and the development of "a wide circle of friends and acquaintances. . . ."[83]

Most Old Regulars accepted this advice. The machine politicos belonged to a wide variety of social, fraternal and benevolent organizations. Fifty-six Regular Democrats, for instance, were Masons. Percy S. Benedict, Joseph D. Taylor and Charles F. Buck were pastmasters of their respective lodges.[84] The Benevolent and Protective Order of Elks was without question the most popular group among Regular Democrats. One hundred twenty-nine Old Regulars were Elks. John P. Sullivan, to cite an outstanding example, was the Exalted Ruler of New Orleans Lodge No. 30. Victor

82.   Brian Gary Ettinger, "John Fitzpatrick and the Limits of Working-Class Politics in New Orleans, 1892-1896," *Louisiana History*, XXVI (Fall 1985), p. 348. See also Chapter 2.
83.   Kemp, ed., *Martin Behrman of New Orleans*, p. 60. See also Zink, *City Bosses*, p. 331.
84.   *Combined Rosters of City Lodges, F. and A. M.* (New Orleans, 1914), *passim*.

Mauberret was a charter member of the Lodge.[85]

Regular Democrats, like local reformers, were also members of the most prestigious clubs in the Crescent City. Thirty-three members of the Choctaw Club belonged to the Boston Club, forty-five politicos belonged to the Pickwick Club and seventy-three belonged to the Chess, Checkers and Whist Club (See Table 27). Lamar C. Quintero was one of several Old Regulars who belonged to all three social clubs. At the start of the twentieth century, he was secretary of the Pickwick Club.[86] Old Regulars were also prominent in the various Mardi Gras krewes. William Mehle and Charles Janvier were former monarchs in the exclusive Rex organization and Paul Capdevielle had been the king of Comus, an even older krewe. In 1902, William McLellan Fayssoux and George Penrose were the captains of Rex and Comus, respectively.[87]

For many Regular Democrats, particularly those who had pulled themselves up by their bootstraps, membership in these exclusive organizations was a satisfying capstone to their business, professional and political achievements. For the Regular Democratic Organization, the presence of its members among the social elite illustrated the broad power base that the urban political machine enjoyed. Because the

85. See *Souvenir Program: Elks Burlesque Circus* (New Orleans, 1906). This publication includes membership rosters.

86. In 1902, a significant number of the Regular Democrats who belonged to the prestigious local men's clubs were former charter members of the Citizens' League. Eight former Citizens' Leaguers who became Old Regulars were members of the Boston Club, twelve belonged to the Pickwick Club and eleven were members of the Chess, Checkers and Whist Club. These recent converts to machine politics certainly enhanced the politicos' presence in the foremost New Orleans social organizations. See *Membership Roster of New Orleans Clubs, 1899*, no pagination; *New Orleans Chess, Checkers and Whist Club* (New Orleans, 1912 and 1913), pp. 42-75; Stuart O. Landry, *History of the Boston Club* (New Orleans 1938), pp. 220-259; Augusto P. Miceli, *The Pickwick Club of New Orleans* (New Orleans, 1964), pp. 190-225.

87. *Times-Picayune*, August 14, 1922, February 18, 1930; "Choctaw Club," pp. 24, 44; Fortier, *Louisiana*, III, 349-352.

Crescent City political organization included bankers, attorneys, physicians and high government officials as well as municipal clerks, flag makers and representatives of the laboring classes, the Regular Democrats received loyal support from a varied constituency and extended powerful tentacles into a multitude of local activities. These extensive interlocking social, business and professional networks smacked of cronyism, but they enabled the professional politicians to amass sizable campaign funds and to maintain their mastery at the polls. This diversity of supporters was unquestionably the key to the Regular Democrats' political success.[88]

The strength of the Old Regulars, of course, did not stop at the city limits. The New Orleans machine exhibited a commanding voice in state government and, through its many nonresident members, exercised political clout in numerous outlying parishes. J. R. Terhune, a representative of Western Union Telegraph; John McGuire, local supervisor for the Southern Pacific Railroad and Sidney H. March, a Crescent City businessman with substantial interests in Alabama, were men of influence. Although he made his residence in Detroit, Brainard Rorison, a charter member of the Choctaw Club who, with Frank P. Mullen, managed the Barber Asphalt Paving Company in New Orleans, advanced the reach of the Regular Democratic Organization beyond the Pelican State. Lamar C. Quintero, legal counsel for the United Fruit Company, and Albert Breton, an agent for the Comptoir National D'Escompte de Paris, bestowed upon the New Orleans political machine international connections.[89]

Power, however, was not the only aim of the Regular Democrats. The New Orleans politicos also sought stabil-

88. Reynolds, *Machine Politics in New Orleans*, pp. 138-161.
89. "Choctaw Club," pp. 6-10, 29, 50; Democratic Party, *The Convention of '98*, p. 37; *Soards, 1898*, p. 702; *Soards' 1900*, pp. 152, 570; *Times-Picayune*, October 31, 1921.

ity.[90] During the last decade of the nineteenth century, the Louisiana port was a volatile town that often erupted in violence. This turbulence was also apparent in local politics. In 1892, the question of, whether or not to extend the charter of the Louisiana State Lottery Company had split the Democratic Party. Although John Fitzpatrick, machine candidate for mayor and a backer of the gambling interests, won the mayoral race, many Regular Democrats shifted their support to the oppositon. When scandal surfaced within the Fitzpatrick administration, foes of the city machine again increased their numbers. In 1896, these opponents of the municipal ring formed the Citizens' League of New Orleans, aligned with a Republican-Populist coalition and employed an appeal for reform to win the municipal elections.[91]

The staggering defeat for the professional politicians prompted reorganization and induced the Regular Democrats to eliminate from the voting ranks, in their minds, the core of the opposition's strength, black citizens. In 1898, the resurgent Old Regulars dominated the New Orleans delegation at a Democrat-dominated constitutional convention that effectively disfranchised blacks and many poor white farmers who had backed the Populist-Republican alliance. At the same time, the convention delegates carefully protected the voting rights of Italian immigrants, traditional supporters of the Democratic machine. Martin Behrman later recalled that "the regular organization came out of the convention in fine shape." In 1899, Crescent City reform elements, deprived of their political allies and racked with internal dissension, crumbled and the Regulars rushed to victory in city elections. The way was clear for decades of

90. For the contributions of political machines to urban stability, see Goldfield and Brownell, *Urban America*, pp. 285-286; Chudacoff, *The Evolution of American Urban Society*, pp. 144-149.

91. Jackson, *New Orleans in the Gilded Age*, pp. 111-135, 137-142, 312-318. See also Chapter 2.

Democratic success. Behrman readily admitted that the poll tax "proved a considerable benefit to us for some time after."[92]

The accomplishment of the Regular Democrats in local affairs was evident on two counts. After 1900, social turmoil in New Orleans generally subsided. Italians began to play a larger role in the city machine, and they made great strides toward assimilation. The subjugation of blacks through segregation and disfranchisement, moreover, apparently reduced white animosity toward blacks and contributed to a reduction in racial violence. In 1922, Martin Behrman observed in his memoirs that the Robert Charles riot of 1900 "was the last occurrence of the kind in New Orleans and all of us are glad of it." The Algiers leader further noted that "the relations between the whites and the blacks are such here today that I do not think it possible for our white people to form mobs and kill negroes [sic] who have committed no offense beyond simply being negroes [sic]."[93]

The greatest testament to the magnitude of the Regular Democrats' achievement, however, was their ability to absorb their former foes. By 1902, the lottery controversy was a dead issue and the Choctaw Club of Louisiana included thirty-one former advocates of the Anti-Lottery League.[94] Perhaps more impressive, however, was the movement of

92. Kemp, ed., *Martin Behrman of New Orleans*, p. 55. See also Kousser, *The Shaping of Southern Politics*, p. 152-165.

93. Kemp, ed. *Martin Behrman of New Orleans*, p. 71. For the rise of Italians in New Orleans politics, see, for example, Edward F. Haas, "New Orleans on the Half-Shell: The Maestri era, 1936-1946," *Louisiana History*, XIII (Summer 1972), pp. 283-310. For the impact of disfranchisement and segregation upon social stability, see Dewey W. Grantham, *Southern Progressivism: The Reconciliation of Progress and Tradition* (Knoxville, 1983), pp. 112-127; George M. Frederickson, "Panic in the South," *The New York Review of Books*, XXXI (December 6, 1984), pp. 28-30.

94. Berthold C. Alwes, "The History of the Louisiana State Lottery Company, *Louisiana Historical Quarterly*," XXVII (October 1927), pp. 1054, 1056, 1105-1109; "Choctaw Club," pp. 6-10. See also *Official Report of the Proceedings of the Anti-Lottery Democratic Convention Held in the Hall of the House of Representatives, Baton Rouge, La. on Thursday and Friday, August 7 and 8, 1890* (New Orleans, 1890), *passim*.

leading members of the Citizens' League into the machine ranks. In 1902, twenty-seven ex-reformers, including Charles Janvier, founder and president of the good government group, belonged to the Choctaw Club. Janvier, Mayor Paul Capdevielle, City Treasurer George Penrose, State Senator Orris L. McLellan, businessman Louis Grunewald and the others were important individuals who greatly strengthened the Old Regulars. For these reform leaders, the shift to the Democratic camp showed the logic of expediency. Since these men ably represented the interests of the local business community, shared the fundamental racial views of the Old Regulars and, with the disintegration of the Republican-Populist-reform coalition, had no suitable political alternatives if they hoped to have a voice in local matters, it was logical to align themselves with the Regular Democrats of New Orleans. They, like their new political partners, were men of stability and influence.[95]

95. "Choctaw Club," pp. 7-10; *Daily Picayune*, December 13, 17, 1896, December 31, 1899; Nussbaum, "Progressive Politics in New Orleans," pp. 202-210. For the limited political alternatives of the former members of the Citizens' League, see Reynolds, *Machine Politics in New Orleans*, pp. 33, 224-227, 230. The charter members of the Citizens' League who joined the Choctaw Club of Louisiana were Percy S. Benedict, George W. Booth, Hugh C. Cage, Capdevielle, James J. Clark, Peter Cougot, Richard H. Downing, Thomas J. Duggan, Samuel L. Gilmore, Jules A. Grasser, Grunewald, Janvier, James W. Kelly, Quitman Kohnke, Joseph A. Littlefield, Theodore H. Lyons, Bernard McCloskey, McLellan, Henry Maspero, T. Marshall Miller, Thomas J. Moran, Penrose, Frank E. Rainold, Walter B. Sommerville, John St. Paul, William G. Turner and John R. Todd. See also Kendall, *History of New Orleans*, II, 532-534.

# V

# Conclusions

In the early twentieth century, the electoral potential of the major Crescent City political factions was inherent in the respective composition of the Citizens' League of New Orleans and the Choctaw Club of Louisiana. Although the Citizens' League included some of the wealthiest and most socially prominent men in the southern metropolis, the reformers were political neophytes. Many had never participated in a political campaign or won public office before the municipal elections of 1896. The Citizens' Leaguers, furthermore, could not repeat their electoral successes. Members of the city's social and financial elite, the good government advocates could never broaden their popular appeal nor could they develop a viable political organization. After the reform debacle of 1899, few Citizens' Leaguers ever again held an elected governmental position.[1] Those who did pursue political careers often shifted alliances. By 1902, the Choctaw Club of Louisiana included within its ranks twenty-seven former members of the reform faction. Among these ex-Citizens' Leaguers were Mayor Paul Capdevielle, State Senator Orris I. McLellan, Justice Walter B. Sommerville of the Louisiana Supreme Court, New Orleans City Attorney Samuel L. Gilmore, New Orleans City Treasurer George B. Penrose and Charles Janvier, a member of the Democratic State Central Committee.[2] Adolph G. Ricks was not a member of the Choctaw Club in 1902, but he later joined the political group when he served on the New Orleans Commission Council during the administration of Mayor Martin Behrman.[3]

1. See Chapter 3.
2. "Choctaw Club," pp. 6-10.
3. *Times-Picayune*, December 16, 1925.

John M. Parker was the most notable former Citizens' Leaguer to remain true to the colors of reform and still pursue a successful political career. In 1912, he backed the Good Government League and then joined the Progressive Party. After four years in the Bull Moose fold, Parker returned to the Democratic ranks. In 1920, he won election to the governorship and actively opposed the Regular Democratic Organization in New Orleans. Parker endorsed the successful mayoral campaign of Andrew McShane over Behrman, the incumbent. McShane, however, was an ineffective leader. In 1925, he lost a reelection bid to Behrman, his old adversary. Parker, though a more successful public official and political strategist than McShane, served only one term as governor and then virtually retired from politics. After Parker and McShane left office, the Old Regulars once more asserted themselves and retained political power in the Crescent City until the election of Huey Long.[4]

The Regular Democrats, conversely, were political professionals who maintained a tight network of ward and precinct organizations. The Regulars occasionally lost elections to their reform opponents, but they never lost sight of their political need to be in close touch with their constituents. Ward leaders and precinct bosses provided that essential contact with the voters. The Regulars, furthermore, sought a broad base of popular support. Although the Choctaw Club, like the reform faction, included the socially and the financially prominent among its members, carpenters, clerks, bartenders and draymen also held influential positions in the New Orleans machine.[5]

These men and their colleagues were political realists who recognized the need for flexibility. When the Regular Democrats lost the municipal elections of 1896, John Fitzpatrick and the other ward leaders wasted little time in reorganizing their forces and soon eliminated a major element in the

4. Schott, "John M. Parker of Louisiana," pp. 384-389. See also Schott, "John Milliken Parker," p. 955.
5. See Chapter 4.

Republican-Populist-reform coalition that had defeated the machine, the black voter. When several key members of the Citizens' League abandoned the reform faction, the Old Regulars welcomed them into the Choctaw Club of Louisiana.[6]

Machine leaders such as Martin Behrman were also willing to adopt many of the ex-Citizens' Leaguers' ideas on business and municipal reform. During the early twentieth century, the New Orleans machine, previously a strong ally of labor, supported local business interests.[7] The politicos also became more receptive to the progressive programs that the reformers advocated. During the Behrman administration, for example, municipal officials completed a public belt railroad, a project that reformers had endorsed since the 1890s. They also improved municipal services and adopted the commission-council form of government.[8]

John Fitzpatrick, Martin Behrman, John Brewster and their allies had fashioned a formidable political organization. Its success was manifest in the four consecutive terms that Martin Behrman served as Crescent City chief executive. Behrman often boasted that he could send down the word on the night before an election and swing 25,000 votes behind any candidate or issue that he chose. This ability made the Regular Democratic Organization of New Orleans into the strongest urban political machine in the South.[9]

The unity that the Regular Democrats exercised over Crescent City voters and the ties that New Orleans politicos developed with their rural counterparts, often nonresident members of the Choctaw Club, also raised the urbanites to a position of great influence in state affairs. The Old Regu-

6.  See Chapter 2.
7.  Reynolds, *Machine Politics in New Orleans*, pp. 138-161.
8.  Kemp, ed., *Martin Behrman of New Orleans*, p. xxiii; Reynolds, *Machine Politics in New Orleans*, pp. 105-106; Robert W. Williams, Jr., "Martin Behrman and New Orleans Civic Development, 1904-1920," *Louisiana History*, II (Fall 1961), pp. 373-400; *Daily Picayune*, October 2, 1912.
9.  Williams, *Huey Long*, p. 130; Sindler, *Huey Long's Louisiana*, pp. 22-23.

lars used their voting strength in the Crescent City and their associations with rural politicians to control the state legislature, the Democratic State Central Committee and many gubernatorial elections. During the first two decades of the twentieth century, the governor of Louisiana was more often than not the choice of the urban machine.[10]

Stability and continuity also contributed to the statewide influence of the Choctaw Club. By 1900, most of the components of the Louisiana conservative oligarchy that had controlled state politics in the last quarter of the nineteenth century were gone or in sharp decline. The Louisiana State Lottery Company was already dead. Major Edward A. Burke, the lottery's chief political manipulator, had taken refuge in Honduras. Disfranchisement had reduced the power of the big planters who no longer had pliant black voters to control. Convict-leasing was on the way out.

The sole exception to this vital political transformation in Louisiana was the Crescent City Democratic machine. The Old Regulars of New Orleans continued to hold sway over their urban electorate and maintained close alliances with politicos in the outlying parishes. When the owners of the lumber mills, the utility corporations, the railroads and the great oil companies rushed to provide fresh conservative leadership after 1900, the New Orleans machine constituted the essential glue that held the new conservative oligarchy together. In a time of political flux, stability, experience, flexibility, and a dependable power base were tremendous assets to the Choctaw Club. From 1899 until the election of Huey Long, the political organization that Fitzpatrick, Behrman, Dudenhefer, Brewster and the New Orleans ward bosses had crafted was the most powerful force in Louisiana politics, a monument to their political acumen.[11]

10.  Sindler, *Huey Long's Louisiana*, pp. 22-23.
11.  Taylor, *Louisiana: A Bicentennial History*, pp. 139, 145-146, 149; Sindler, *Huey Long's Louisiana*, pp. 22-24.

# FIGURES AND TABLES

# FIGURE 1

## New Orleans Political Organizations and Clubs: 1868-1899

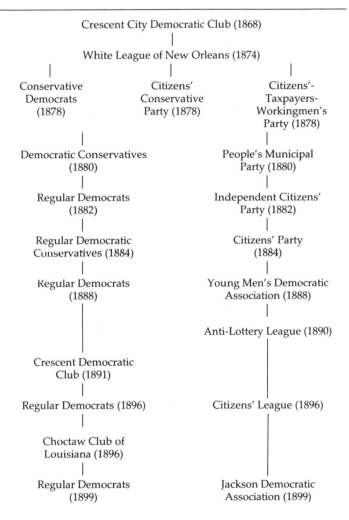

Crescent City Democratic Club (1868)

White League of New Orleans (1874)

| Conservative Democrats (1878) | Citizens' Conservative Party (1878) | Citizens'-Taxpayers-Workingmen's Party (1878) |

Democratic Conservatives (1880)

People's Municipal Party (1880)

Regular Democrats (1882)

Independent Citizens' Party (1882)

Regular Democratic Conservatives (1884)

Citizens' Party (1884)

Regular Democrats (1888)

Young Men's Democratic Association (1888)

Anti-Lottery League (1890)

Crescent Democratic Club (1891)

Regular Democrats (1896)

Citizens' League (1896)

Choctaw Club of Louisiana (1896)

Regular Democrats (1899)

Jackson Democratic Association (1899)

# TABLE 1

## Regular Ward Leaders

| WARD | APRIL 1896 | SEPTEMBER 1899 |
|------|-----------|----------------|
| 1 | C. Taylor Gauche <br> Mike Fanning | C. Taylor Gauche <br> Mike Fanning |
| 2 | Thomas Reynolds <br> Robert C. Davey | Robert C. Davey |
| 3 | John Fitzpatrick <br> Remy Klock | Remy Klock |
| 4 | Victor Mauberret | Victor Mauberret |
| 5 | Alfred Barnes | Alexander Pujol* |
| 6 | John Brewster | John Brewster |
| 7 | Louis Knop | P. A. Capdau <br> Louis Knop |
| 8 | Joseph Hirn | Joseph Hirn |
| 9 | Ferdinand <br> Dudenhefer | Ferdinand <br> Dudenhefer |
| 10 | Peter Farrell | Robert Ewing |
| 11 | George C. Preot | J. A. Malloy* |
| 12 | H. B. McMurray | H. B. McMurray |
| 13 | A. F. Michel | John T. Michel |
| 14 | B. T. Walshe | Samuel L. Gilmore |
| 15 | T. J. Mooney | Martin Behrman <br> T. J. Mooney |
| 16 | O. A. Trezevant | O. A. Trezevant |
| 17 | W. H. Willett | Fred Deibel |

* chosen successor
SOURCE: *Daily Picayune,* April 6, 1896, September 9, 1899

# TABLE 2

Citizens' League
Birthplace of Charter Members
(N = 235)

| BIRTHPLACE | NUMBER | PERCENTAGE |
|---|---|---|
| Known | 230 | 97.9 |
| Louisiana | 145 | 63.0 |
| (New Orleans) | (108) | (47.0) |
| South | 40 | 17.4 |
| Northeast | 10 | 4.4 |
| Midwest | 7 | 3.0 |
| West | 0 | 0.0 |
| Ireland | 14 | 6.1 |
| Germany | 6 | 2.6 |
| England | 5 | 2.2 |
| France | 2 | 0.9 |
| Switzerland | 1 | 0.4 |
| Unknown | 5 | 2.1 |

# TABLE 3

Citizens' League
Immigrant Parentage of Native-Born Charter Members
(N = 188)

| PARENTS' ORIGINS | NUMBER | PERCENTAGE |
|---|---|---|
| Known | 188 | 100.0 |
| Immigrant Parent(s) | 92 | 48.9 |
| Native-born Parents | 96 | 51.1 |
| Unknown | 0 | 0.0 |

# TABLE 4

**Citizens' League**
**Birthplace of Fathers of Native-Born Charter Members**
**(N = 202)**

| BIRTHPLACE | NUMBER | PERCENTAGE |
|---|---|---|
| Known | 188 | 93.1 |
| Louisiana | 41 | 21.8 |
| South | 42 | 22.4 |
| Northeast | 19 | 10.1 |
| Midwest | 2 | 1.1 |
| West | 0 | 0.0 |
| Ireland | 29 | 15.4 |
| Germany | 21 | 11.2 |
| France | 16 | 8.5 |
| England | 5 | 2.7 |
| Spain | 6 | 3.2 |
| Austria | 1 | 0.5 |
| Scotland | 2 | 1.1 |
| Sweden | 1 | 0.5 |
| Canada | 1 | 0.5 |
| Martinique | 1 | 0.5 |
| Santo Domingo | 1 | 0.5 |
| Unknown | 14 | 6.9 |

# TABLE 5

**Citizens' League**
**Birthplace of Mothers of Native-Born Charter Members**
**(N = 202)**

| BIRTHPLACE | NUMBER | PERCENTAGE |
|---|---|---|
| Known | 188 | 93.1 |
| Louisiana | 61 | 32.5 |
| South | 41 | 21.7 |
| Northeast | 15 | 8.0 |
| Midwest | 2 | 1.1 |
| West | 0 | 0.0 |
| Ireland | 30 | 16.0 |
| Germany | 15 | 8.0 |
| France | 11 | 5.9 |
| England | 5 | 2.6 |
| Scotland | 3 | 1.6 |
| Spain | 1 | 0.5 |
| Sweden | 1 | 0.5 |
| Martinique | 2 | 1.1 |
| Cuba | 1 | 0.5 |
| Unknown | 14 | 6.9 |

## TABLE 6

### Citizens' League
### Residence Distance from City Core of the Charter
### Members
### (N = 235)

| BLOCK RADIUS | NUMBER | PERCENTAGE |
|---|---|---|
| Known | 235 | 100.0 |
| 1-9 blocks | 19 | 8.1 |
| 10-19 blocks | 58 | 24.7 |
| 20-29 blocks | 64 | 27.2 |
| 30-39 blocks | 38 | 16.2 |
| 40-49 blocks | 14 | 6.0 |
| 50-59 blocks | 12 | 5.1 |
| 60-69 blocks | 17 | 7.2 |
| 70-79 blocks | 1 | 0.4 |
| Over 80 blocks | 7 | 3.0 |
| Algiers | 4 | 1.7 |
| St. Bernard | 1 | 0.4 |
| Unknown | 0 | 0.0 |

## TABLE 7

### Citizens' League
### Residence Direction of the Charter Members
### (N = 235)

| RESIDENCE | NUMBER | PERCENTAGE |
|---|---|---|
| Known | 235 | 100.0 |
| Uptown from Canal Street | 182 | 77.4 |
| Downtown from Canal Street | 48 | 20.5 |
| Algiers | 4 | 1.7 |
| St. Bernard | 1 | 0.4 |
| Unknown | 0 | 0.0 |

# TABLE 8

## Citizens' League
## Ward Residence of the Charter Members
## (N = 235)

| WARD | NUMBER | PERCENTAGE |
|---|---|---|
| Known | 235 | 100.0 |
| First | 15 | 6.4 |
| Second | 16 | 6.8 |
| Third | 16 | 6.8 |
| Fourth | 7 | 3.0 |
| Fifth | 10 | 4.3 |
| Sixth | 12 | 5.1 |
| Seventh | 15 | 6.4 |
| Eighth | 1 | 0.4 |
| Ninth | 3 | 1.3 |
| Tenth | 32 | 13.6 |
| Eleventh | 35 | 14.9 |
| Twelfth | 25 | 10.6 |
| Thirteenth | 13 | 5.5 |
| Fourteenth | 22 | 9.4 |
| Fifteenth | 4 | 1.7 |
| Sixteenth | 4 | 1.7 |
| Seventeenth | 4 | 1.7 |
| St. Bernard | 1 | 0.4 |
| Unknown | 0 | 0.0 |

## TABLE 9

Citizens' League
Date of birth of the Charter Members
(N = 235)

| BIRTHDATE | NUMBER | PERCENTAGE |
|---|---|---|
| Known | 232 | 98.7 |
| 1820-1829 | 5 | 2.2 |
| 1830-1839 | 20 | 8.6 |
| 1840-1849 | 54 | 23.3 |
| 1850-1859 | 75 | 32.3 |
| 1860-1869 | 67 | 28.9 |
| 1870-1879 | 11 | 4.7 |
| Unknown | 3 | 1.3 |

## TABLE 10

Citizens' League
Occupations of the Charter Members
(N = 235)

| OCCUPATION | NUMBER | PERCENTAGE |
|---|---|---|
| Known | 235 | 100.0 |
| Business | 161 | 68.5 |
| Professional | 66 | 28.1 |
| (Law) | (45) | (19.2) |
| (Medicine) | (18) | (7.7) |
| (Engineering) | (0) | (0.0) |
| (Education) | (1) | (0.4) |
| (Journalism) | (2) | (0.9) |
| Skilled labor | 7 | 3.0 |
| Unskilled labor | 1 | 0.4 |
| Unknown | 0 | 0.0 |

## TABLE 11

Citizens' League
**Education of the Charter Members**
**(N = 235)**

| EDUCATIONAL LEVEL | NUMBER | PERCENTAGE |
|---|---|---|
| Known | 140 | 59.6 |
| Professional and/or | | |
| Postgraduate | 52 | 37.2 |
| College | 23 | 16.4 |
| Secondary | 22 | 15.7 |
| Elementary | 37 | 26.4 |
| Business School | 6 | 4.3 |
| Unknown | 95 | 40.4 |

## TABLE 12

Citizens' League
**Taxable Wealth of the Charter Members**
**(N = 235)**

| WEALTH | NUMBER | PERCENTAGE |
|---|---|---|
| Known | 160 | 68.1 |
| $1-1,000 | 23 | 14.4 |
| $1,001-2,500 | 20 | 12.5 |
| $2,501-5,000 | 24 | 15.0 |
| $5,001-10,000 | 22 | 13.7 |
| $10,001-25,000 | 36 | 22.5 |
| $25,001-50,000 | 18 | 11.3 |
| $50,001-100,000 | 8 | 5.0 |
| over $100,000 | 9 | 5.6 |
| Unknown | 75 | 31.9 |

## TABLE 13

Citizens' League
Religion of the Charter Members
(N = 235)

| RELIGION | NUMBER | PERCENTAGE |
|---|---|---|
| Known | 133 | 56.6 |
| Catholic | 74 | 55.6 |
| Protestant | 53 | 39.8 |
| Jewish | 6 | 4.5 |
| Unknown | 102 | 43.4 |

## TABLE 14

Citizens' League
Organizational Membership of the Charter Members
(N = 235)

| ORGANIZATION | NUMBER | PERCENTAGE |
|---|---|---|
| White League | 30 | 12.8 |
| Volunteer fire department | 6 | 2.6 |
| Elks | 31 | 13.2 |
| Masons | 35 | 14.9 |
| Boston Club | 76 | 32.3 |
| Pickwick Club | 42 | 17.9 |
| Chess, Checkers and Whist Club | 72 | 30.6 |

## TABLE 15
### Birthplace of the Regular Democrats
### (N = 407)

| BIRTHPLACE | NUMBER | PERCENTAGE |
|---|---|---|
| Known | 396 | 97.3 |
| Louisiana | 291 | 73.5 |
| (New Orleans) | (195) | (49.2) |
| South | 26 | 6.5 |
| Northeast | 14 | 3.5 |
| Midwest | 8 | 2.0 |
| West | 1 | 0.3 |
| Ireland | 14 | 3.5 |
| Germany | 13 | 3.3 |
| England | 6 | 1.5 |
| France | 5 | 1.3 |
| Italy | 4 | 1.0 |
| Canada | 5 | 1.3 |
| Mexico | 2 | 0.5 |
| Other Foreign | 7 | 1.8 |
| Unknown | 11 | 2.7 |

## TABLE 16
### Immigrant Parentage of Native-Born Regular Democrats
### (N = 340)

| PARENTS' ORIGINS | NUMBER | PERCENTAGE |
|---|---|---|
| Known | 334 | 98.2 |
| Immigrant Parent(s) | 191 | 57.1 |
| Native-born Parents | 143 | 42.9 |
| Unknown | 6 | 1.8 |

## TABLE 17
### Birthplace of Fathers of Native-Born Regular Democrats
### (N = 340)

| BIRTHPLACE | NUMBER | PERCENTAGE |
|---|---|---|
| Known | 334 | 98.2 |
| Louisiana | 93 | 27.8 |
| South | 31 | 9.3 |
| Northeast | 25 | 7.5 |
| Midwest | 7 | 2.0 |
| West | 0 | 0.0 |
| Ireland | 60 | 18.0 |
| Germany | 51 | 15.3 |
| France | 36 | 10.8 |
| England | 10 | 3.0 |
| Scotland | 4 | 1.2 |
| Italy | 3 | 0.9 |
| Spain | 3 | 0.9 |
| Canada | 3 | 0.9 |
| Switzerland | 2 | 0.6 |
| Other Foreign | 6 | 1.8 |
| Unknown | 6 | 1.8 |

# TABLE 18

**Birthplace of Mothers of Native-Born Regular Democrats**
**(N = 340)**

| BIRTHPLACE | NUMBER | PERCENTAGE |
| --- | --- | --- |
| Known | 334 | 98.2 |
| Louisiana | 134 | 40.1 |
| South | 27 | 8.1 |
| Northeast | 17 | 5.1 |
| Midwest | 6 | 1.8 |
| West | 0 | 0.0 |
| Ireland | 70 | 21.0 |
| Germany | 45 | 13.5 |
| France | 18 | 5.4 |
| England | 8 | 2.4 |
| Spain | 2 | 0.5 |
| Scotland | 2 | 0.5 |
| Other Foreign | 5 | 1.5 |
| Unknown | 6 | 1.8 |

## TABLE 19
### Residence Distance from the City Core of the Regular Democrats
### (N = 407)

| BLOCK RADIUS | NUMBER | PERCENTAGE |
|---|---|---|
| Known | 402 | 98.8 |
| 1-9 blocks | 40 | 10.0 |
| 10-19 blocks | 133 | 33.1 |
| 20-29 blocks | 109 | 27.1 |
| 30-39 blocks | 37 | 9.2 |
| 40-49 blocks | 37 | 9.2 |
| 50-59 blocks | 14 | 3.5 |
| 60-69 blocks | 14 | 3.5 |
| 70-79 blocks | 7 | 1.7 |
| 80-89 blocks | 4 | 1.0 |
| Algiers | 7 | 1.7 |
| Unknown | 5 | 1.2 |

## TABLE 20
### Residence Direction of the Regular Democrats
### (N = 407)

| RESIDENCE DIRECTION | NUMBER | PERCENTAGE |
|---|---|---|
| Known | 403 | 99.0 |
| Uptown from Canal Street | 265 | 65.8 |
| Downtown from Canal Street | 131 | 32.5 |
| Algiers | 7 | 1.7 |
| Unknown | 4 | 1.0 |

## TABLE 21

**Ward Residence of the Regular Democrats**
**(N = 407)**

| WARD | NUMBER | PERCENTAGE |
|---|---|---|
| Known | 403 | 99.0 |
| First | 29 | 7.2 |
| Second | 31 | 7.7 |
| Third | 56 | 13.9 |
| Fourth | 28 | 7.0 |
| Fifth | 25 | 6.2 |
| Sixth | 26 | 6.5 |
| Seventh | 25 | 6.2 |
| Eighth | 15 | 3.7 |
| Ninth | 12 | 3.0 |
| Tenth | 42 | 10.4 |
| Eleventh | 24 | 6.0 |
| Twelfth | 36 | 8.9 |
| Thirteenth | 17 | 4.2 |
| Fourteenth | 22 | 5.5 |
| Fifteenth | 7 | 1.7 |
| Sixteenth | 5 | 1.2 |
| Seventeenth | 3 | 0.7 |
| Unknown | 4 | 1.0 |

## TABLE 22
### Date of Birth of the Regular Democrats
### (N = 407)

| DATE OF BIRTH | NUMBER | PERCENTAGE |
|---|---|---|
| Known | 397 | 97.5 |
| 1820-1829 | 2 | 0.5 |
| 1830-1839 | 14 | 3.5 |
| 1840-1849 | 68 | 17.1 |
| 1850-1859 | 122 | 30.7 |
| 1860-1869 | 119 | 30.1 |
| 1870-1879 | 69 | 17.4 |
| 1880-1889 | 3 | 0.7 |
| Unknown | 10 | 2.5 |

## TABLE 23
### Occupational Backgrounds of the Regular Democrats
### (N = 407)

| OCCUPATION | NUMBER | PERCENTAGE |
|---|---|---|
| Known | 402 | 98.8 |
| Business | 242 | 60.2 |
| Professional | 119 | 29.6 |
| (Law) | (83) | (20.7) |
| (Medicine) | (9) | (2.2) |
| (Engineering) | (18) | (4.5) |
| (Education) | (5) | (1.2) |
| (Journalism) | (4) | (1.0) |
| Skilled labor | 33 | 8.2 |
| Unskilled labor | 8 | 2.0 |
| Unknown | 5 | 1.2 |

# TABLE 24

## Education of the Regular Democrats
## (N = 407)

| EDUCATIONAL LEVEL | NUMBER | PERCENTAGE |
|---|---|---|
| Known | 194 | 47.7 |
| Professional and/or | | |
| Postgraduate | 73 | 37.6 |
| College | 34 | 17.5 |
| Secondary | 38 | 19.6 |
| Elementary | 43 | 22.2 |
| Business School | 6 | 3.1 |
| Unknown | 213* | 52.3 |

* The large number of unknowns in Table 24 indicates that many Regular Democrats had limited formal educations.

# TABLE 25

## Taxable Wealth of the Regular Democrats
## (N = 407)

| WEALTH | NUMBER | PERCENTAGE |
|---|---|---|
| Known | 194 | 47.7 |
| $1-1,000 | 20 | 10.3 |
| $1,001-2,500 | 35 | 18.0 |
| $2,501-5,000 | 52 | 26.8 |
| $5,001-10,000 | 41 | 21.1 |
| $10,001-25,000 | 30 | 15.5 |
| $25,001-50,000 | 10 | 5.2 |
| $50,001-100,000 | 4 | 2.1 |
| over $100,000 | 2 | 1.0 |
| Unknown | 213 | 52.3 |

## TABLE 26
### Religion of the Regular Democrats
### (N = 407)

| RELIGION | NUMBER | PERCENTAGE |
| --- | --- | --- |
| Known | 215 | 52.8 |
|   Catholic | 161 | 74.9 |
|   Protestant | 48 | 22.3 |
|   Jewish | 6 | 2.8 |
| Unknown | 192 | 47.2 |

## TABLE 27
### Organizational Memberships of the Regular Democrats
### (N = 407)

| ORGANIZATION | NUMBER | PERCENTAGE |
| --- | --- | --- |
| White League | 25 | 6.1 |
| Volunteer Fire Department | 53 | 13.0 |
| Elks | 129 | 31.7 |
| Masons | 56 | 13.8 |
| Boston Club | 33 | 8.1 |
| Pickwick Club | 45 | 11.1 |
| Chess, Checkers and Whist Club | 73 | 17.9 |
| Anti-Lottery League | 31 | 7.6 |
| Citizens' League of New Orleans | 27 | 6.6 |

# APPENDIX 1
## Biographical Information on the Citizens' League of New Orleans

| NAME | YEAR OF BIRTH | PLACE OF BIRTH | IMMIGRANT PARENT(S) | 1897 RESIDENCE (DISTANCE FROM CITY CORE IN BLOCKS) | 1897 OCCUPATION | 1897 WEALTH | EDUCATION | RELIGION |
|---|---|---|---|---|---|---|---|---|
| Jacob H. Abraham | 1865 | La. | yes | 39U | cotton merchant | 9,200 | S | J |
| Frederick Adolph | 1855 | La. (N.O.) | yes | 46U | notary, lawyer | | P | Pr |
| Martin Alleyn | 1843 | La. (N.O.) | yes | 22U | real estate | 300 | S | Ca |
| Paul E. Archinard | 1858 | La. (N.O.) | | 15D | physician | 6,900 | P | Ca |
| Johnston Armstrong | 1863 | Ky. | | 22U | attorney | 2,550 | P | Pr |
| Louis G. Arnauld | 1836 | La. | | 12D | judge | | | |
| Charles Ballejo | 1837 | La. (N.O.) | yes | 24U | grocer | 8,700 | | Ca |
| Frank Barker | 1852 | La. | | 19D | commission merchant | 22,300 | E | |
| Hugh A. Bayne | 1870 | La. | | 31U | attorney | 41,000 | P | |
| Thomas L. Bayne | 1865 | La. (N.O.) | | 31U | real estate | 1,200 | C | |
| E. L. Bemiss | | | | SB | water, electric | 900 | | |
| Percy S. Benedict* | 1871 | La. (N.O.) | | 20U | attorney | 13,000 | P | Pr |
| George H. Bernos | 1871 | La. (N.O.) | yes | 36D | sugar broker | 1,000 | | |
| Henry Bezou | 1825 | La. | | 12D | merchant, insurance, judge | | C | |
| Joseph P. Blair | 1859 | Ms. | | 26U | attorney | | P | Pr |
| George W. Booth* | 1851 | La. (N.O.) | yes | 16U | business agent | 4,600 | C | Pr |
| Edward Bothe | 1859 | La. (N.O.) | | 12D | painter, court clerk | | | |
| Henry C. Boucher | 1822 | Va. | yes | 7D | retail merchant | 34,300 | | |
| Julian S. Boullemet | 1857 | La. | | 31U | saddler | 90 | | Pr |
| B. Winchester Bowling | 1860 | La. | | 29U | dry goods merchant | 8,000 | | |
| Joseph C. Boylan | 1866 | La. (N.O.) | yes | 12U | newspaper dealer | 17,700 | | |

| NAME | YEAR OF BIRTH | PLACE OF BIRTH | IMMIGRANT PARENT(S) | 1897 RESIDENCE (DISTANCE FROM CITY CORE IN BLOCKS) | 1897 OCCUPATION | 1897 WEALTH | EDUCATION | RELIGION |
|---|---|---|---|---|---|---|---|---|
| Sidney Bradford | 1862 | La. (N.O.) | | 18U | coal merchant | 1,750 | P | |
| George C. Bright | 1841 | Ak. | | 14U | clerk | 3,500 | | Pr |
| Abraham Britton | | | | 7U | cotton broker, councilman | | S | Pr |
| William Brophy | 1868 | La. (N.O.) | yes | 20U | grocer, councilman | 3,405 | E | Ca |
| H. Dickson Bruns | 1859 | S.C. | | 23U | physician | | P | |
| Lucien N. Brunswig | 1854 | France | | 26U | wholesale druggist | 142,300 | | |
| Louis P. Bryant | 1856 | La. (N.O.) | yes | 17D | attorney | 2,700 | | Pr |
| Nicholas Burke | 1834 | Ireland | | 58U | grocer | 127,250 | | |
| Reuben G. Bush | 1854 | La. | | 22U | commission merchant | 7,700 | | Ca |
| John G. Bryd | 1835 | | | 19D | insurance | | | |
| William H. Byrnes | 1846 | Ireland | | 21U | insurance | | S | Ca |
| Hugh C. Cage* | 1859 | La. | | 62U | attorney | 4,800 | P | |
| Aloysius J. Cahill | 1869 | La. | yes | 33U | attorney | | | Ca |
| Paul Capdevielle* | 1842 | La. | yes | 29D | insurance | | | Ca |
| Leigh Carroll | 1862 | La. (N.O.) | | 17U | water, electric | | P | |
| David B. H. Chaffe | 1864 | La. (N.O.) | | 45U | attorney | 1,800 | C | |
| Stanford E. Chaille | 1830 | Ms. | | 4U | physician | 39,300 | P | |
| Charles Chassaignac | 1862 | La. (N.O.) | yes | 11U | physician | 2,400 | P | |
| James J. Clark* | 1860 | La. (N.O.) | yes | 25U | grocer | 27,150 | P | Pr |
| Louis Claudel | 1859 | La. | yes | 17D | optician | 4,000 | E | Ca |
| Peter Clement | 1852 | La. | | A | carpenter, judge | 700 | E | Ca |

| Name | Year | Place | | Code | Occupation | Value | | |
|---|---|---|---|---|---|---|---|---|
| Peter Cougot* | 1868 | La. (N.O.) | yes | 13D | real estate, insurance | | | |
| Edward Couturie | 1858 | La. (N.O.) | yes | 28D | broker | 200 | S | Ca |
| Felix Couturie | 1858 | La. (N.O.) | yes | 24D | cotton broker | 48,500 | S | Ca |
| Robert E. Craig | 1842 | Ms. | yes | 24U | water works president | | | |
| Charles H. Culbertson | 1860 | La. (N.O.) | | 36U | bank cashier | | | Ca |
| Frank Dameron | 1862 | La. (N.O.) | | 34U | stationer | | S | |
| Michael Delucas | 1856 | La. (N.O.) | yes | 81U | court clerk, collector | 3,100 | E | |
| Justin F. Denechaud | 1863 | La. (N.O.) | yes | 3U | hotel owner | | B | |
| George Denegre | 1856 | La. (N.O.) | | 31U | attorney | 58,300 | P | Ca |
| Walter Denegre | 1858 | La. (N.O.) | | 23U | attorney | | P | Ca |
| George W. Dinkel | 1859 | La. (N.O.) | yes | 3D | collector | | E | |
| Joseph S. Doane | 1855 | La. (N.O.) | | 23U | clerk | | E | |
| William E. Dodsworth | 1857 | La. | yes | 48U | tax clerk | 2,500 | | |
| Richard H. Downing* | 1862 | La. | yes | 51U | attorney, judge | 2,500 | S | Ca |
| Christopher Doyle | 1851 | Ireland | | 59U | grocer | 60,650 | | |
| Felix J. Dreyfous | 1857 | La. (N.O.) | yes | 25U | attorney, notary | 20,915 | P | J |
| Charles W. Drown | 1849 | La. | yes | 16U | railroad treasurer | 4,000 | | Ca |
| William C. Dufour | 1871 | La. (N.O.) | | 7U | attorney | 3,800 | P | |
| Thomas J. Duggan* | 1867 | Va. | yes | 14U | attorney, levee board secretary | 425 | P | Ca |
| Michael F. Dunn | 1842 | La. (N.O.) | yes | 45U | stationer | 18,250 | | Ca |
| William H. Dwyer | 1870 | La. (N.O.) | yes | 52U | notions | 42,400 | | Ca |
| Isadore Dyer | 1865 | Tx. | yes | 20U | physician | | P | |
| George Eike | 1844 | La. (N.O.) | yes | 16D | merchant, councilman | 19,350 | E | Ca |

| NAME | YEAR OF BIRTH | PLACE OF BIRTH | IMMIGRANT PARENT(S) | 1897 RESIDENCE (DISTANCE FROM CITY CORE IN BLOCKS) | 1897 OCCUPATION | 1897 WEALTH | EDUCATION | RELIGION |
|---|---|---|---|---|---|---|---|---|
| John B. Elliott | 1841 | S.C. | | 24U | physician | | | |
| Thomas S. Ellis | 1870 | La. (N.O.) | | 53U | attorney | | P | |
| Benjamin F. Eshleman | 1830 | Pa. | | 29U | hardware | 167,800 | | Ca |
| Edward J. Faure | 1867 | La. (N.O.) | | 17U | secretary | | | |
| Charles Feahney | 1857 | Fla. | | 8U | grocer | 20,500 | E | |
| Charles P. Fenner | 1867 | Ms. | | 27U | attorney | | P | Ca |
| Erasmus D. Fenner | 1868 | La. | | 27U | physician, assistant coroner | 35,000 | P | Pr |
| Gabriel Fernandez | 1847 | La. (N.O.) | | 12D | attorney, judge | | P | Ca |
| George R. Finlay | 1835 | Ireland | | 46U | druggist | 750 | E | |
| Edward Finnegan | 1842 | Ireland | | 21U | clerk | | E | Ca |
| Andrew Fitzpatrick | 1871 | La. (N.O.) | yes | 16U | attorney, insurance, hides dealer | 33,300 | P | Ca |
| Horace Fletcher | 1849 | | | 4U | manager | | | |
| Walter C. Flower | 1850 | La. | | 19U | cotton broker, mayor | 34,100 | P | Pr |
| Hugh Flynn | 1830 | Ireland | | 10U | furniture dealer | 41,400 | | Ca |
| Edward P. Foley | 1864 | La. (N.O.) | yes | 21U | attorney, constable | 800 | | Ca |
| B. B. Sims Folwell | 1865 | La. (N.O.) | | 8U | collector, court clerk | | C | Ca |
| Edward P. Fournier | 1858 | Al. | | 46U | bookkeeper | | | |
| Joseph Fromherz | 1849 | La. (N.O.) | yes | 30U | builder | 6,600 | | Ca |
| Joseph Garcia | 1846 | La. (N.O.) | yes | 24D | stationer | 10,075 | | Ca |

| Name | | Origin | | | Occupation | | | |
|---|---|---|---|---|---|---|---|---|
| Samuel Garic | 1856 | La. (N.O.) | | 14D | bakery owner | 28,250 | E | |
| Charles Garvey | | | | 6D | builder | | | |
| Paul J. Gelpi | 1847 | La. (N.O.) | yes | 18D | liquor dealer | 3,500 | S | Ca |
| John T. Gibbons | 1837 | Md. | yes | 13U | grain, insurance | 49,725 | | Ca |
| Peter J. Gillen | 1851 | N.Y. | yes | 16U | bookkeeper | | E | Ca |
| Samuel L. Gilmore* | 1858 | La. (N.O.) | yes | 61U | attorney | 9,500 | P | Ca |
| August Glaudot, Jr. | 1864 | La. (N.O.) | yes | 21D | tobacco dealer | | C | Ca |
| Isaac E. Glenny | 1828 | England | | 62U | cotton broker | 24,500 | | Pr |
| David Glover | 1847 | Ireland | | 23U | bagging dealer | 15,000 | | |
| William A. Gordon | 1858 | La. (N.O.) | yes | 18U | commission merchant | 15,500 | | |
| Joseph M. Gore | 1858 | La. | | 54U | bookkeeper | 3,300 | E | Ca |
| Jules A. Grasser* | 1876 | La. (N.O.) | yes | 20U | attorney | 2,720[1] | S | Pr |
| Gilbert H. Green | 1851 | Va. | yes | 35U | bank clerk | | S | Ca |
| John A. Grehan | 1851 | La. | yes | 27U | warehouse clerk | | | Ca |
| Louis Grunewald* | 1828 | Germany | | 15U | hotel owner, music dealer | 455,355 | | |
| Paul O. Guerin | 1847 | La. (N.O.) | | 30D | court clerk | | E | |
| Louis Guillaud | 1844 | France | | A | undertaker, councilman | 2,000 | | |
| Horace Gumbel | 1865 | La. | yes | 23U | broker | | | J |
| William J. Hannon | 1864 | La. | yes | 21D | ship carpenter | 4,600 | | Ca |
| Edward Harper | 1842 | La. (N.O.) | yes | 80U | grocer, judge | | | |
| James L. Harris | 1866 | La. (N.O.) | yes | 28D | clerk | | | |
| Frank B. Hayne | 1858 | S.C. | | 60U | cotton merchant | 700 | | Ca |
| Samuel F. Heaslip | 1846 | England | | 26U | boss drayman | 10,000 | S | |
| Otto Helmann | 1861 | La. (N.O.) | yes | 34U | druggist, councilman | 16,450 | E | |

| NAME | YEAR OF BIRTH | PLACE OF BIRTH | IMMIGRANT PARENT(S) | 1897 RESIDENCE (DISTANCE FROM CITY CORE IN BLOCKS) | 1897 OCCUPATION | 1897 WEALTH | EDUCATION | RELIGION |
|---|---|---|---|---|---|---|---|---|
| Erasmus F. Henderson | 1860 | La. (N.O.) | | 40U | insurance | 82,875 | | Pr |
| Samuel Henderson, Jr. | 1863 | Ga. | | 62U | attorney | 700 | P | Pr |
| Patrick F. Hennessey | 1860 | La. (N.O.) | | A | attorney, judge | | P | Ca |
| Joseph F. Herberger | 1858 | La. (N.O.) | yes | 37U | grocer, tanner, councilman | 2,080 | E | |
| Isadore Hernsheim | 1847 | Ms. | | 39U | fire alarm merchant | 63,750 | B | |
| Frederick T. Holderith | 1863 | La. (N.O.) | | 31U | paint works owner | | | |
| Charles Janvier* | 1857 | La. (N.O.) | | 62U | insurance | 16,400 | C | Ca |
| James G. Jenkins | 1849 | Ia. | | 62U | ice company owner | | E | Pr |
| J. Wallace Johnson | 1858 | La. (N.O.) | | 9D | insurance | | C | Ca |
| Charles S. Judson | 1858 | La. (N.O.) | | 34U | clerk | | | |
| James W. Kelly* | 1863 | La. (N.O.) | yes | 16U | recorder of mortgages | 2,800 | E | |
| Edward F. Kohnke | 1849 | Ms. | yes | 15U | flour merchant | 7,600 | | Ca |
| Quitman Kohnke* | 1857 | Ms. | yes | 16U | physician, councilman | 125 | P | Ca |
| William H. Krone | 1856 | Germany | | 28U | builder | 21,900 | | Ca |
| John W. Labouisse | 1841 | La. (N.O.) | | 61U | cotton broker | 3,000 | C | Ca |
| R. Henry Labouisse | 1867 | N.Y. | | 43U | cotton merchant | 3,700 | | |
| J. Henry Lafaye | 1843 | La. (N.O.) | | 37D | commission merchant | 3,700 | E | Ca |
| Orloff Lake | 1855 | Md. | | 61U | manufacturer | 4,600 | C | |
| Horatio Lange | 1855 | La. (N.O.) | yes | 16D | stockbroker | 13,500 | | Pr |

| | | | | | | | | |
|---|---|---|---|---|---|---|---|---|
| Wesley E. Lawrence | 1854 | Ma. | | 72U | commission merchant | 84,300 | P | |
| Richard H. Lea | 1858 | Mn. | | 85U | attorney, cotton exchange secretary | | | Pr |
| George M. Leahy | 1857 | La. (N.O.) | yes | 11U | stockbroker | 1,600 | P | Pr |
| Louis G. Leboeuf | 1865 | La. | | 27U | physician | 150 | S | |
| Fergus G. Lee | 1862 | La. (N.O.) | | 29D | insurance | 2,350 | P | Pr |
| Yves R. Lemonnier | 1845 | La. (N.O.) | | 14D | physician, coroner | | C | Ca |
| John B. Levert | 1836 | La. | | 25U | merchant | 14,300 | | Ca |
| Jonas M. Levy | 1847 | Ms. | yes | 12U | cotton factor | | P | |
| Ernest S. Lewis | 1840 | La. (N.O.) | yes | 7U | physician | 19,150 | B | |
| George Lhote | 1855 | La. (N.O.) | yes | 11D | manufacturer | 6,450 | E | Ca |
| Joseph A. Littlefield* | 1857 | La. (N.O.) | yes | 21U | stockbroker | 2,275[2] | | Pr |
| Henry Lochte | 1845 | Germany | | 81U | grocer, councilman | 161,525 | | |
| Clarence F. Low | 1854 | La. (N.O.) | | 22U | insurance | 4,000 | C | |
| William R. Lyman | 1838 | N.Y. | | 84U | insurance | 11,950 | E | Pr |
| Isaac L. Lyons | 1837 | S.C. | | 22U | wholesale druggist | 258,500 | P | Pr |
| Lucien E. Lyons | 1856 | S.C. | | 34U | pharmacist | 10,700 | | Pr |
| Theodore H. Lyons* | 1850 | S.C. | | 33U | wholesale druggist | 13,200 | | Pr |
| Bernard McCloskey* | 1860 | Ireland | | 7U | attorney | 2,000 | P | Ca |
| Hugh McCloskey | 1853 | Ireland | | 31U | grocer, commission merchant | 33,100 | E | Ca |
| John McCloskey | 1848 | Ireland | | 18U | confectioner | 81,675 | | Ca |
| Patrick McCloskey | 1860 | Ireland | | 7U | commission merchant | 14,000 | E | Ca |
| William L. McGary | 1861 | Ky. | | 29U | insurance | 550 | E | |
| Scott McGehee | 1843 | Ms. | | 34U | insurance | | E | |

| NAME | YEAR OF BIRTH | PLACE OF BIRTH | IMMIGRANT PARENT(S) | 1897 RESIDENCE (DISTANCE FROM CITY CORE IN BLOCKS) | 1897 OCCUPATION | 1897 WEALTH | EDUCATION | RELIGION |
|---|---|---|---|---|---|---|---|---|
| John McGraw | 1859 | La. (N.O.) | | 62U | merchant | 5,500 | E | Pr |
| Orris I. McLellan* | 1853 | La. (N.O.) | | A | dock company president | 128,900 | | |
| William C. McLeod | 1866 | La. (N.O.) | yes | 61U | attorney | 50 | P | |
| James L. McLoughlin | 1860 | La. (N.O.) | yes | 60U | attorney, assistant city attorney | 10,600 | P | Ca |
| Albert Mackie | 1858 | La. | yes | 40U | grocer | 52,525 | | |
| Otto T. Maier | 1866 | La. | yes | 22D | insurance | 1,500 | | |
| Frank Marquez | 1841 | La. (N.O.) | yes | 19D | cotton inspector, civil sheriff | 7,550 | C | |
| Robert H. Marr | 1861 | La. (N.O.) | | 34U | district attorney | 16,600 | P | |
| Leon Martiny | 1857 | La. (N.O.) | yes | 18D | clerk, constable | | | |
| Henry Maspero* | 1859 | La. (N.O.) | | 12D | stockbroker | | B | |
| George Mather | 1847 | La. | | 35U | cotton broker | | | |
| George B. Matthews | 1857 | Mo. | | 33U | merchant | 26,300 | | |
| Herman Meader | 1841 | Prussia | | 49U | grocer, councilman | 94,600 | E | Pr |
| Samuel B. Merwin | 1859 | La. | | 52U | boss drayman | | | |
| Eugene Mestier | 1848 | La. (N.O.) | yes | 7D | commercial travel | | S | Ca |
| T. Marshall Miller* | 1847 | Ms. | | 22U | attorney | 8,500³ | P | Pr |
| Frank D. Mitchell | 1853 | La. | yes | 34U | salesman | | | |
| William J. Montgomery | 1860 | Ms. | | 25U | grocer | | C | Pr |
| George W. Moore | 1872 | La. | yes | 69U | attorney | 1,000 | P | |
| Thomas J. Moran* | 1845 | La. (N.O.) | yes | 15U | stationer | 19,700 | | Ca |
| John A. Muir | 1836 | La. (N.O.) | yes | 19U | architect, councilman | 1,500 | S | Pr |

| Name | Year | Origin | | Age | Occupation | Value | | |
| --- | --- | --- | --- | --- | --- | --- | --- | --- |
| John W. Murphy | 1863 | La. (N.O.) | yes | 13U | tarpaulin dealer, commissioner of public buildings | 1,200 | C | Ca |
| Leonard Naef | 1852 | Switzerland | | 81U | grain merchant, councilman | 28,750 | | Pr |
| W. O'Reardon | 1845 | Ireland | | 4U | merchant | | | |
| Frederick A. Ober | 1840 | Al. | | 23U | insurance | 1,500 | | Pr |
| Frank S. Palfrey | 1857 | La. (N.O.) | | 21U | insurance | | E | |
| James R. Parker | 1845 | La. | | 39U | cotton planter | 2,000 | S | |
| John M. Parker | 1863 | Ms. | | 46U | cotton factor, grocer | 17,000 | | Pr |
| Porter Parker | 1870 | Ms. | | 25U | attorney | | P | Pr |
| Robert B. Parker | 1869 | La. | | 8U | grocer | | C | Pr |
| George B. Penrose* | 1857 | La. (N.O.) | | 23U | city treasurer | 750 | C | Ca |
| Emilien Perrin | 1866 | La. (N.O.) | | 46U | stockbroker | 15,000 | E | Ca |
| John W. Phillips | 1848 | Al. | | 26U | druggist | 9,250 | | |
| William F. Pinckard | 1847 | Ms. | | 26U | cotton broker | 16,100 | | |
| Gustave Pitot | 1838 | La. (N.O.) | | 12D | seltzer dealer | | | Ca |
| William J. Pollard | 1840 | Ga. | | 8U | broker | | | |
| Henry M. Preston | 1843 | Il. | yes | 21U | grocer | 162,750 | | Ca |
| Felix Puig | 1868 | La. (N.O.) | | 5D | attorney | 18,300 | P | Ca |
| P. Alphonse Rabouin | 1848 | La. (N.O.) | | 19D | notary, city comptroller | 1,300 | E | |
| William M. Railey | 1861 | La. (N.O.) | | 61U | insurance | 23,300 | E | |
| John Scott Rainey | 1847 | La. (N.O.) | | 26U | chemicals | | | J |
| Frank E. Rainold* | 1865 | La. | yes | 22U | attorney | 12,100 | P | Pr |
| Paul S. Reiss | 1867 | La. | yes | 23D | oculist | | P | Pr |
| Ferdinand Reusch, Jr. | 1860 | La. (N.O.) | yes | 21U | builder | 32,775 | B | Ca |

| NAME | YEAR OF BIRTH | PLACE OF BIRTH | IMMIGRANT PARENT(S) | 1897 RESIDENCE (DISTANCE FROM CITY CORE IN BLOCKS) | 1897 OCCUPATION | 1897 WEALTH | EDUCATION | RELIGION |
|---|---|---|---|---|---|---|---|---|
| Joseph M. Rice | 1848 | England | | 13U | commission merchant | 6,550 | | Ca |
| William R. Richardson | 1852 | La. (N.O.) | yes | 17U | judge, attorney | 5,650 | P | Ca |
| Adolph G. Ricks | 1842 | Germany | | 21U | leather goods, councilman | 22,100 | E | Pr |
| John St. Paul* | 1867 | Al. | yes | 29D | attorney | | P | Ca |
| Matthew J. Sanders | 1859 | England | | 61U | steamship agent | 12,000 | | Pr |
| Dennis Sheen | 1845 | Ireland | | 32D | boss drayman | 7,700 | | |
| John M. Sherrouse | 1848 | La. | | 55U | merchant, councilman | 9,100 | E | |
| James Simeon | 1866 | La. | yes | 62U | notary | 2,000 | | |
| James B. Sinnott | 1840 | Ireland | | 29U | merchant | | S | Ca |
| William Sirjacques | 1862 | La. (N.O.) | yes | 11U | lumber dealer | 500 | E | |
| Walter B. Sommerville* | 1854 | La. (N.O.) | | 35U | assistant city attorney | 4,500 | P | |
| Edward J. Soniat | 1852 | La. (N.O.) | | 18D | sugar broker | 5,700 | E | |
| Cohn M. Soria | 1830 | N.Y. | yes | 31U | grain merchant | 49,650 | P | |
| George Soule | 1834 | N.Y. | | 30U | commercial college president | 16,500 | | Pr |
| Walker B. Spencer | 1868 | Ms. | | 33U | attorney | | P | Pr |
| John Stanley | 1858 | La. (N.O.) | yes | 26D | clerk, registrar of conveyances | 2,350 | E | Ca |
| Thomas J. Stanton | 1861 | La. (N.O.) | yes | 13U | corn merchant | 6,850 | B | Ca |
| Walter R. Stauffer | 1854 | La. (N.O.) | | 21U | hardware merchant | 173,050 | | Ca |

| Name | Year | Birthplace | | Age | Occupation | Wealth | | |
|---|---|---|---|---|---|---|---|---|
| Maurice Stern | 1855 | Germany | | 50U | cotton factor | 800 | E | J |
| Henry Stewart | 1862 | Ak. | | 11U | cotton broker | | S | Pr |
| Sidney Story | 1863 | La. (N.O.) | | 12D | journalist, councilman | | C | |
| Edward J. Thilberger | 1860 | La. (N.O.) | yes | 42U | attorney, judge | | P | Ca |
| John F. Tobin | 1871 | La. (N.O.) | | 28D | attorney | | P | Pr |
| Edward Toby | 1831 | La. (N.O.) | yes | 18U | banker | 100 | S | |
| Simon Toby | 1828 | La. (N.O.) | yes | 38U | journalist | | C | Pr |
| John R. Todd* | 1842 | La. (N.O.) | | 16U | manufacturer's agent | 1,500 | E | Pr |
| Hippolyte Tosso | 1843 | La. (N.O.) | yes | 10D | hardware dealer | 8,000 | S | |
| William G. Turner* | 1856 | Ws. | yes | 44U | cotton press owner | | C | |
| William E. Uniacke | 1861 | Ms. | yes | 15D | painter, sheriff | 4,450 | P | |
| George J. Untereiner | 1868 | La. (N.O.) | yes | 33U | attorney | | | |
| George A. Villere | 1854 | La. (N.O.) | | 32U | merchant | | | |
| Robert M. Walmsley | 1833 | Md. | | 25U | banker | | S | Pr |
| Matthew Warriner | 1859 | England | | 84U | steamship agent | 5,800 | | |
| Patrick Westfeldt | 1855 | N.Y. | | 25U | coffee dealer | 400 | C | Pr |
| Robert Whann | 1851 | Oh. | yes | 39U | coal merchant | 10,300 | | |
| August B. Wheeler | 1854 | La. (N.O.) | | 68U | banker | 34,000 | | Pr |
| Burris D. Wood | 1836 | Pa. | | 51U | merchant | 600 | | Pr |
| Elmer E. Wood | 1861 | Pa. | | 54U | merchant | 15,600 | C | Pr |
| Samuel E. Worms | 1853 | La. | | 36U | banker, notions | 15,850 | E | J |
| James J. Woulfe | 1860 | La. (N.O.) | yes | 19U | city notary | 50 | C | Ca |
| George W. Young | 1848 | La. (N.O.) | yes | 57U | banker | 4,600 | S | Ca |

APPENDIX NOTES:

1. 1902 wealth.
2. 1902 wealth.
3. 1900 wealth.

KEY: In the listings above, the asterisk (*) indicates that the person was a member of the Choctaw Club in 1902. The abbreviations have the following meanings: U-Uptown above Canal Street; D-Downtown below Canal Street; A-Algiers; SB-St. Bernard; E-Elementary education; S-Secondary education; B-Business school; C-College education; P-Professional and/or graduate education; Ca-Catholic; Pr-Protestant; J-Jewish.

SOURCES: Manuscript Census Returns, Tenth Census of the United States, 1880; Twelfth Census of the United States, 1900; Thirteenth Census of the United States, 1910; Louisiana, Orleans Parish, Records of the United States Bureau of the Census; City of New Orleans Real Estate Tax Ledgers, 1896-1897, 1900-1902; *Soards' New Orleans City Directory*, 1896-1910; *Tulane News Bulletin*, 1921-1930; *The Citizens' League: A History of the Great Reform Movement in New Orleans*, April 21, 1896 (New Orleans, n. d.); "Choctaw Club of Louisiana," *Club Life*, Special Edition (May 1902); New Orleans press, especially *Daily Picayune*, 1896-1914; *Times-Democrat*, 1896-1914; *Times-Picayune*, 1914-1954; *Daily States*, 1896-1954; *Item*, 1896-1954; and various other primary and secondary sources, published and unpublished.

# APPENDIX 2
## Biographical Information on the Regular Democratic Organization of New Orleans

| NAME | YEAR OF BIRTH | PLACE OF BIRTH | IMMIGRANT PARENT(S) | 1900 RESIDENCE (DISTANCE FROM CITY CORE IN BLOCKS) | 1900 OCCUPATION | 1902 WEALTH | EDUCATION | RELIGION |
|---|---|---|---|---|---|---|---|---|
| Sturges Adams* | 1880 | La. (N.O.) | | 23U | court stenographer | | P | |
| Samuel J. Alston* | 1837 | La. (N.O.) | | 28U | cashier | | E | Pr |
| Thomas C. Anderson* | 1858 | La. | yes | 15D | oil company owner | 17,000 | E | Ca |
| Henry Andry† | 1848 | La. (N.O.) | | 7D | court clerk | | | |
| William Appolino* | 1875 | La. (N.O.) | yes | 13D | clerk | | | Ca |
| William Ardill† | 1863 | Cuba | | 17D | notary | | | Ca |
| Henry Armbruster* | 1840 | Germany | | 25U | oil, brewing | 26,750 | | |
| Theodore Atchison* | 1866 | Ky. | | 7U | attorney | 100[1] | | |
| August Aucoin* | 1845 | La. | | 14D | judge | | P | |
| Charles E. Babcock* | 1846 | La. (N.O.) | | 41U | tax clerk | | | Pr |
| John Calhoun Bach† | 1838 | La. (N.O.) | | 35U | stockbroker | 16,685[2] | C | Ca |
| Joshua Baker* | 1852 | La. | | 19U | judge | | S | |
| James Barnett* | 1860 | La. (N.O.) | yes | 15U | legislator, clerk | | S | Ca |
| George F. Bartley* | 1876 | La. (N.O.) | | 14U | attorney | | P | Ca |
| James M. Batchelor* | 1871 | La. | | 11U | physician | | P | Pr |
| Charles Bedell* | 1856 | La. (N.O.) | yes | 21U | ironworks owner | 2,000 | E | |
| Martin Behrman†* | 1864 | N.Y. | yes | A | assessor | 1,800[3] | B | Ca |
| Percy S. Benedict* | 1871 | La. (N.O.) | | 20U | attorney | 15,200 | P | |
| Leon Benedito† | 1854 | La. (N.O.) | yes | 12D | saloon manager | | | |
| Charles Benson* | 1834 | Ireland | | 24U | carriage maker | 19,000 | | |
| Frederick Bertrand* | 1842 | Canada | | 36D | bar proprietor | | | Ca |
| John A. Beta* | 1845 | La. (N.O.) | yes | 3U | flag maker | 450 | | |
| Frank E. Bishop† | 1859 | La. (N.O.) | yes | 21U | police commissioner | 1,500 | E | Ca |

| NAME | YEAR OF BIRTH | PLACE OF BIRTH | IMMIGRANT PARENT(S) | 1900 RESIDENCE (DISTANCE FROM CITY CORE IN BLOCKS) | 1900 OCCUPATION | 1902 WEALTH | EDUCATION | RELIGION |
|---|---|---|---|---|---|---|---|---|
| Achille Blais* | 1866 | La. (N.O.) | yes | 33D | government clerk | | S | Ca |
| Peter A. Blaise* | 1838 | Germany | | 15U | brewing | 50,875[4] | | Ca |
| George W. Booth* | 1851 | La. (N.O.) | yes | 16U | capitalist | 3,350 | C | Pr |
| A. L. Bourgeois† | 1870 | La. | | A | barber | | | |
| John T. Brady† | 1866 | Ireland | | 25D | blacksmith | | | Ca |
| William J. Brady* | 1872 | La. (N.O.) | yes | 16U | government clerk | | S | Ca |
| Edward A. Brandao† | 1847 | La. | yes | 55U | bookkeeper | | | |
| Anthony G. Brasco* | 1846 | Italy | | 2U | restaurant owner | 2,000 | | Ca |
| Louis Brehm* | 1871 | La. | yes | 81U | court clerk | 11,200 | | |
| Ambrose J. Brennan* | 1853 | La. (N.O.) | yes | 27U | clerk | | | Ca |
| Albert Breton* | 1866 | France | | 15D | bank cashier | | | |
| John Brewster* | 1836 | Ireland | | 17D | tax collector | 23,600 | | Ca |
| George H. Brockman* | 1862 | Md. | yes | 24D | stenographer | 3,600[5] | | |
| Daniel M. Brosnan* | 1849 | N.Y. | yes | 31U | civil engineer | 6,800[6] | C | Pr |
| E. D. Brown* | 1847 | | | | | | | |
| Linus W. Brown* | 1856 | N.Y. | | 7U | civil engineer | 8,100 | S | |
| Charles H. Brownlee* | 1853 | La. (N.O.) | yes | A | court clerk | | P | |
| Charles Brunning* | 1863 | La. | yes | 15D | physician | 22,200 | | |
| Henry J. Brunning* | 1860 | La. | yes | 15D | attorney | 11,350 | P | |
| A. M. Buchmann* | 1871 | La. (N.O.) | | 21D | attorney | | P | Ca |
| Charles F. Buck* | 1841 | Germany | | 48U | attorney | 65,000 | C | |
| Joseph T. Buddecke* | 1872 | La. | yes | 55U | government clerk | | C | Ca |
| William Bulger* | 1845 | La. (N.O.) | yes | 12U | special officer | | | |
| Charles A. Byrne* | 1873 | La. (N.O.) | yes | 8U | court stenographer | | P | Ca |

| Name | Year | Place | | Code | Occupation | Wealth | | |
|---|---|---|---|---|---|---|---|---|
| Hugh C. Cage* | 1859 | La. | | 52U | attorney | 4,900 | P | |
| Joseph V. Calhoun* | 1837 | Pa. | | 16U | education | 5,500 | C | Ca |
| Joseph V. Calhoun, Jr.* | 1864 | La. (N.O.) | | 16U | superintendent | | | Ca |
| George Califat† | 1862 | La. | yes | 13U | bookkeeper | | | |
| James F. Cannon* | 1859 | La. (N.O.) | | 18U | bartender | | | |
| Gustave Cantrelle* | 1868 | La. (N.O.) | | 6D | wagondriver | | | |
| Pierre A. Capdau* | 1863 | La. (N.O.) | yes | 28D | government clerk | 15,500 | S | Ca |
| Paul Capdevielle* | 1842 | La. (N.O.) | yes | 29D | druggist | | P | Ca |
| Thomas J. Carey† | 1864 | La. (N.O.) | yes | 13U | mayor, insurance | | P | Ca |
| George W. Chaery† | 1857 | La. | yes | 14D | deputy sheriff | | | Ca |
| Henry Chiapella* | 1847 | La. (N.O.) | | 19D | clerk[7] | | | |
| Frank Chretien† | 1849 | La. | | 17D | attorney | 3,500 | P | Ca |
| James J. Clark* | 1860 | La. (N.O.) | yes | 25U | attorney, judge | 3,500 | C | Ca |
| John Clegg* | 1852 | N.C. | | 27U | grocer | 6,800 | E | Ca |
| Edward D. Cobb† | 1828 | Md. | | 3D | attorney | | P | Pr |
| J. Frank Coleman* | 1866 | Ms. | | 22U | clerk[8] | | | |
| Charles J. Colton† | 1868 | La. (N.O.) | | 27D | civil engineer | | S | Pr |
| Thomas W. Connell* | 1865 | La. (N.O.) | yes | 13U | stenographer | | E | Ca |
| John H. Conniff* | 1850 | La. (N.O.) | yes | 41U | court clerk | | | Ca |
| John R. Conniff* | 1874 | La. (N.O.) | | 41U | journalist | 10,900 | E | Pr |
| Edward L. Cope* | 1840 | England | | 24D | teacher | | P | Pr |
| Charles W. Corson† | 1852 | La. | | 4JU | port | 5,100[9] | E | Ca |
| Peter Cougot† | 1868 | La. (N.O.) | yes | 13D | superintendent | | | |
| Pierre Crabites* | 1878 | La. (N.O.) | yes | 11U | stationer | | | |
| William T. Crotts* | 1863 | Ind. | | 13U | real estate | 48,825 | P | Ca |
| James M. Cullen† | 1871 | La. (N.O.) | yes | 13U | attorney | 1,600[10] | | Ca |

Additional occupations noted: civil engineer, drug clerk

| NAME | YEAR OF BIRTH | PLACE OF BIRTH | IMMIGRANT PARENT(S) | 1900 RESIDENCE (DISTANCE FROM CITY CORE IN BLOCKS) | 1900 OCCUPATION | 1902 WEALTH | EDUCATION | RELIGION |
|---|---|---|---|---|---|---|---|---|
| Michael E. Culligan* | 1855 | La. (N.O.) | yes | 15U | clerk | 800 | E | Ca |
| Charles Cuneo* | 1849 | Italy | | 19D | court clerk | 2,800 | | Ca |
| John Dahmer* | 1845 | Germany | | 77U | machinist | 2,000 | | |
| John J. Darrieux* | 1872 | La. | yes | 15D | attorney | 2,500 | P | Ca |
| John C. Davey, Jr.* | 1880 | La. (N.O.) | | 9U | attorney | | C | Ca |
| Robert C. Davey* | 1853 | La. (N.O.) | yes | 11U | United States Congressman | | C | Ca |
| Henry J. Davezact | 1854 | France | | 14D | clerk | | | |
| George Dearmas†* | 1860 | La. (N.O.) | | 15D | surveyor | | | Ca |
| Charles L. Defuentes* | 1844 | La. (N.O.) | | 18D | cotton broker | | C | Ca |
| Pedro Deprida* | 1867 | Mexico | | 16U | | | | |
| Arthur J. Desmond†* | 1846 | La. | yes | 21D | court clerk | | E | |
| Joseph T. Devereux* | 1878 | La. (N.O.) | | 31D | stockbroker | | C | |
| Charles Dickson†* | 1852 | La. (N.O.) | yes | 18U | tarpaulin, lumber, councilman | 20,300 | E | Ca |
| George Dietrich* | 1867 | La. (N.O.) | yes | 42D | tax clerk | 900 | | |
| M. Dracos Dimitry* | 1874 | La. (N.O.) | | 17U | attorney | | P | |
| Joseph W. Dodds* | 1870 | La. | | 25U | train conductor | | | |
| Charles Donnaud* | 1864 | La. | | 22U | police board secretary | | | |
| William S. Douglass* | 1861 | La. | yes | 17U | warehouse treasurer | | | |
| John Dowdle* | | | | 51U[11] | contractor[12] | | | |
| David Dowers† | 1858 | England | | 15U | attorney | 12,490 | | |

| Name | Year | Place | | Age | Occupation | Wealth | | |
|---|---|---|---|---|---|---|---|---|
| Richard H. Downing* | 1862 | La. | yes | 50U | attorney, judge | 3,700 | S | |
| Meyer Dreifus* | 1854 | La. | yes | 6U[13] | prison clerk[14] | | S | |
| Henry R. Ducastaing* | 1858 | La. (N.O.) | yes | 7D | government clerk | | | Ca |
| Paul A. Ducoing* | 1865 | La. | | 18D | court clerk | 200 | S | |
| Ferdinand Dudenhefert* | 1847 | Germany | | 28D | tax clerk | | E | |
| J. M. Duff* | | | | | | | | |
| Thomas J. Duggan* | 1867 | Va. | yes | 44U | accountant[15] levee board secretary | 1,000[16] | P | Ca |
| Theodore Dumas* | 1831 | Canada | | 44U | furniture dealer | 24,450 | S | Pr |
| Adolphe Dumser* | 1858 | La. (N.O.) | yes | 28D | merchant | 9,800 | P | Ca |
| H. Garland Dupre* | 1873 | La. | | 65U | attorney | | | Pr |
| Andre D. Duval* | 1864 | France | | 23D | government engineer | 4,000[17] | | |
| John Dymond, Sr.* | 1836 | Canada | | 27U | sugar, publishing | | C | Pr |
| John Dymond, Jr.* | 1867 | N.Y. | yes | 26U | attorney | | P | Pr |
| Warren Easton* | 1854 | La. (N.O.) | | 26U | education superintendent | | C | Pr |
| Marcelin T. Elfert* | 1849 | La. (N.O.) | yes | 45U | merchant | 7,500 | | |
| Frederick G. Ernst* | 1853 | La. (N.O.) | yes | 27U | merchant | 13,600 | | |
| Robert Ewing† | 1859 | Al. | yes | 24U | journalist | | S | Pr |
| James D. Farrell* | 1860 | La. (N.O.) | yes | 44U | dock commissioner | 2,900 | | |
| Peter Farrell* | 1842 | Ct. | yes | 23U | state coal gauger | 1,800 | S | |
| William C. Faust* | 1848 | La. | yes | 28D | merchant | 16,200 | | |
| William McL. Fayssoux* | 1873 | La. (N.O.) | | 28U | attorney | | P | Pr |
| Maurice Feitel* | 1858 | La. | | 18U | contractor | 4,225 | | |
| Conrad B. Fischer* | 1861 | La. (N.O.) | yes | 73U | lumber merchant | 32,900 | | Ca |
| John Fitzpatrick* | 1844 | Vt. | yes | 13U | tax collector | 33,200 | E | Ca |

| NAME | YEAR OF BIRTH | PLACE OF BIRTH | IMMIGRANT PARENT(S) | 1900 RESIDENCE (DISTANCE FROM CITY CORE IN BLOCKS) | 1900 OCCUPATION | 1902 WEALTH | EDUCATION | RELIGION |
|---|---|---|---|---|---|---|---|---|
| William H. Fitzpatrick* | 1849 | Ireland | | 23U | real estate | 2,400[18] | | Ca |
| Arthur V. Flotte† | 1844 | La. (N.O.) | | 15D | accountant | | E | |
| George W. Flynn†* | 1853 | La. (N.O.) | yes | 21U | attorney | 12,500 | P | Ca |
| Thomas J. Ford†* | 1853 | La. (N.O.) | yes | 16D | attorney | 6,500 | | |
| Pierre Adolph Fortier† | 1832 | La. | | 22D | collector | 50 | | |
| George W. Foster†* | 1866 | La. (N.O.) | yes | A | liquor dealer | 6,400 | S | Ca |
| Paul L. Fourchy† | 1861 | La. (N.O.) | | 31D | attorney | | P | Ca |
| Joseph J. Fowler* | 1848 | Canada | | 20U | government secretary | | | Ca |
| John L. Frawley†* | 1865 | Ms. | yes | 12U | city contractor | 3,500 | | Ca |
| Joseph W. Frellson†* | 1850 | La. | yes | 10D | real estate | 600[19] | | |
| Alexander B. French* | 1843 | England | | 17U | steamship agent | | S | Ca |
| Carl C. Friedrichs* | 1876 | La. (N.O.) | yes | 6U | attorney | | P | Ca |
| Adam Gambel* | 1849 | Germany | | 23D | sugar merchant | 51,450 | | |
| Lionel R. Garcia* | 1852 | La. | | 22U | cotton merchant | 2,700 | | |
| Joseph Garidel* | 1841 | La. (N.O.) | yes | 26D | court clerk | | C | Ca |
| Junios J. Garlick* | 1848 | La. (N.O.) | yes | 20U | bill poster | 1,800 | E | |
| Dexter S. Gaster† | 1844 | Oh. | | 9U | police chief | | | |
| Samuel T. Gately* | 1859 | La. (N.O.) | yes | 41D | marble dealer | 1,600 | E | Ca |
| C. Taylor Gaucher†* | 1844 | La. (N.O.) | yes | 14U | building materials, assessor | 6,000 | E | Ca |
| Daniel J. Geary* | 1862 | La. | yes | 22U | salesman | 600[20] | | |
| Joseph E. Generelly* | 1874 | La. (N.O.) | | 20D | attorney | | P | Ca |
| Charles G. Gill* | 1866 | La. (N.O.) | | 30U | attorney | | P | |

| Name | Year | Origin | | Ward | Occupation | Wealth | | |
|---|---|---|---|---|---|---|---|---|
| Henry M. Gill† | 1872 | La. (N.O.) | | 23U | professor | | C | Pr |
| Thomas M. Gill, Jr.* | 1874 | La. (N.O.) | | 30U | judge | | P | |
| Samuel L. Gilmore* | 1858 | La. (N.O.) | yes | 61U | city attorney | 10,200 | P | Ca |
| Thomas M. Gilmore* | 1843 | Ireland | | 19D | grocer | 7,000 | C | Ca |
| Jesse S. Glass* | 1872 | La. | | 71U | publisher | | | |
| Jeremiah M. Gleason* | 1847 | Ireland | yes | 20U | registrar of voters | 6,500 | E | Ca |
| Walter L. Gleason* | 1877 | Pa. | yes | 20U | attorney | | P | Ca |
| George J. Glover* | 1868 | La. (N.O.) | yes | 58U | contractor | 9,100 | E | Ca |
| John Glynn, Jr.* | 1841 | Ireland | | 15D | assessor | | S | Ca |
| Rudolph J. Goebel* | 1868 | La. (N.O.) | yes | 34D | councilman, restaurant | 11,200 | | Pr |
| Christian M. Goss* | 1852 | La. | yes | 48U | deputy sheriff[21] | 700 | E | Ca |
| Eugene Grasser* | 1870 | La. (N.O.) | yes | 31U | paving contractor | 4,080 | S | Ca |
| Jules A. Grasser* | 1876 | La. (N.O.) | yes | 20U | attorney | 2,750 | | Ca |
| Louis Grunewald* | 1828 | Germany | | 15U | music dealer | 257,450 | | |
| Maxime Guirand* | 1876 | La. (N.O.) | | 38U | tobacco dealer | 1,800 | | |
| Ludwig W. Gunther* | 1877 | La. (N.O.) | yes | 11U | court clerk | | | |
| Charles Hagen† | 1854 | Germany | | 11U | restaurant owner | | | |
| Andrew J. Hamilton* | 1870 | La. | yes | 18U | carpenter | | S | Pr |
| William J. Hardee† | 1863 | Ms. | | 8D | city engineer | | P | |
| William R. Harnant† | 1866 | La. (N.O.) | | 17U | physician[22] | 2,800[23] | S | Pr |
| William O. Hart* | 1857 | La. (N.O.) | | 37U | attorney | 48,650 | C | |
| Joseph O. Hasam* | 1865 | La. | | 43U | civil engineer | | | |
| George A. Hassinger* | 1866 | La. | yes | 22U | rice merchant | 3,000 | | |
| Charles J. Hauer* | 1864 | La. (N.O.) | yes | 23D | saloon keeper | 3,500 | | |
| Alvin Edward Hebert* | 1878 | La. | | 5U | attorney | | P | Ca |
| Charles Heider* | 1851 | Ms. | yes | 16U | harness maker | | | |
| Sydney I. Heineman† | | | | 16U[24] | attorney[25] | | | |

| NAME | YEAR OF BIRTH | PLACE OF BIRTH | IMMIGRANT PARENT(S) | 1900 RESIDENCE (DISTANCE FROM CITY CORE IN BLOCKS) | 1900 OCCUPATION | 1902 WEALTH | EDUCATION | RELIGION |
|---|---|---|---|---|---|---|---|---|
| J. C. Henriques* | 1870 | La. (N.O.) | yes | 54U | attorney | 3,000 | P | |
| Henry G. Hester* | 1846 | La. (N.O.) | yes | 57U | cotton exchange secretary | | S | |
| Joseph Him* | 1844 | Germany | | 22D | barber, assessor | 3,800 | S | |
| Henry Hirsch* | 1873 | Ms. | yes | 17U | merchant | 5,300 | | |
| Harmon Hoey† | 1847 | La. | | 80U | levee foreman | | | Pr |
| Walter H. Hoffman* | 1854 | La. | | 60U | civil engineer | 1,100 | | Ca |
| John C. Hollingsworth* | 1879 | La. | | 32U | clerk | | | |
| Joseph J. Hooper* | 1849 | La. | | 84U | stationer | 2,400 | | |
| Robert L. Hottinger* | 1875 | La. (N.O.) | yes | 45U | daily laborer | | | Ca |
| Henry Hourbeigt† | 1852 | La. | yes | 15U | levee inspector | | | |
| James Hughes* | 1868 | La. (N.O.) | yes | 22U | judge | 4,700 | | Ca |
| William L. Hughes† | 1866 | La. (N.O.) | yes | 16D | attorney | | P | |
| George S. Humphreys* | 1860 | La. (N.O.) | | | manufacturer's agent | | | Ca |
| Thomas McC. Hyman* | 1848 | La. | | 21D | court clerk | | P | Ca |
| Charles J. Jackson* | 1877 | La. (N.O.) | | 43U | clerk | | | |
| Fritz Jahncke* | 1848 | Germany | | 10U | cement merchant | 43,200 | E | |
| Irwin Jamison* | 1861 | La. | yes | 9U | cement contractor | | | |
| Charles Janvier* | 1857 | La. (N.O.) | | 62U | insurance | 13,000 | C | Ca |
| William J. Kane† | 1850 | La. (N.O.) | yes | 21U | blacksmith | 8,650 | | Ca |
| James W. Kelly* | 1863 | La. (N.O.) | yes | 23U | recorder of mortgages | | E | |
| Charles T. Kelsko* | 1856 | Denmark | | 8U | ticket broker | 6,000[26] | | |

| Name | Year | Place | | Age | Occupation | Value | | |
|---|---|---|---|---|---|---|---|---|
| Beauregard Kendall* | 1861 | La. | | 17U | machinist | | | Pr |
| Charles R. Kennedy* | 1853 | La. (N.O.) | | 31D | court constable | 3,500 | S | Ca |
| Patrick J. Kennedy* | 1865 | La. | yes | 28U | postal superintendent | | | |
| Francis J. Kenner* | 1873 | La. | | 21U | solicitor | | | Ca |
| Maurice Kenny* | 1850 | Ireland | | 10U | grocer | 5,000 | | Ca |
| William A. Kernaghan*† | 1832 | La. (N.O.) | yes | 44U | real estate | 1,200 | S | |
| Peter J. Kernan* | 1865 | La. | | 12D | messenger | | | Ca |
| Frank M. Kerr* | 1851 | La. (N.O.) | yes | 8D | state engineer | | P | Pr |
| Douglas M. Kilpatrick* | 1844 | La. (N.O.) | yes | 41U | merchant | | S | Ca |
| Frank W. Kinberger* | 1860 | La. | yes | 15U | grocer | 7,450 | | |
| Frederick D. King* | 1850 | La. | | 32U | attorney, judge | | | |
| John D. R. King, Jr.* | 1873 | Al. | | | court appraiser[27] | | | |
| Walter D. Kingston† | 1859 | La. (N.O.) | yes | 46U | real estate | | | |
| William C. Kirkland* | 1862 | Canada | | 65U | government engineer | | P | |
| Alfred N. Klein* | 1855 | La. | yes | 18U | train conductor | | | Ca |
| Remy Klock† | 1851 | Ky. | yes | 35U | criminal sheriff | 4,600 | E | Ca |
| Samuel J. Kohlman† | 1854 | Ca. | yes | 19U | cotton broker | | | |
| Quitman Kohnke* | 1857 | Ms. | yes | 20U | physician | | P | Ca |
| Ernest B. Kruttschnitt* | 1852 | La. (N.O.) | yes | 24U | attorney | 10,000 | C | Pr |
| Albert L. Lanauze* | 1868 | La. (N.O.) | yes | 18D | cotton clerk | | | Ca |
| P. Henry Lanauze* | 1859 | La. (N.O.) | yes | 18D | board of health registrar | | S | Ca |
| Robert S. Landry*† | 1860 | La. (N.O.) | | 29D | government bookkeeper | 3,000[28] | S | |
| George Willard Lawes* | 1857 | La. (N.O.) | | 74U | government engineer | | S | Ca |

| NAME | YEAR OF BIRTH | PLACE OF BIRTH | IMMIGRANT PARENT(S) | 1900 RESIDENCE (DISTANCE FROM CITY CORE IN BLOCKS) | 1900 OCCUPATION | 1902 WEALTH | EDUCATION | RELIGION |
|---|---|---|---|---|---|---|---|---|
| Henry L. Lazarus* | 1853 | N.Y. | yes | 35U | attorney | | C | J |
| Frank C. Leathers† | 1867 | La. | | 17D | steamboat captain | | C | Ca |
| Adolph S. Leclerc* | 1851 | La. (N.O.) | | 6D | merchant | 13,500 | E | Ca |
| Henry J. Ledoux* | 1866 | La. (N.O.) | | 27D | water merchant | | | Ca |
| Rene LeGardeur† | 1869 | La. (N.O.) | | 31D | bookkeeper | | C | Ca |
| Albert L. Legeai* | 1858 | La. (N.O.) | yes | 20D | postal clerk | 2,700 | | Ca |
| Robert Legier* | 1871 | La. (N.O.) | | 19D | notary, recorder of mortgages | 2,500 | P | Ca |
| Emile Leonard* | 1865 | La. (N.O.) | | 19D | clerk | 4,000[29] | S | Ca |
| Sidney Lewis† | 1854 | La. (N.O.) | | 12D | state engineer | | P | Ca |
| Eugene Limongi* | 1869 | La. (N.O.) | yes | 8D | grocery clerk | | | Ca |
| Felix Limongi† | 1867 | La. (N.O.) | yes | 8D | merchant | | | Ca |
| Joseph A. Littlefield* | 1857 | La. (N.O.) | yes | 21U | stockbroker | 2,275 | E | Pr |
| John H. Littleton* | 1851 | La. | | 21U | detective | 240 | | |
| Matthew J. Long* | 1857 | La. (N.O.) | yes | 15U | government clerk | 2,400 | | Ca |
| Hilaire Loubat* | 1857 | France | | 3D | glass merchant | 5,400 | | |
| Emile Louis* | 1867 | La. (N.O.) | yes | 10D | stenographer | | | Ca |
| James G. Lynch* | 1867 | La. (N.O.) | yes | 11U | court clerk | | S | Ca |
| Theodore H. Lyons* | 1850 | S.C. | | 33U | drug clerk | 13,200 | | Pr |
| E. Howard McCaleb* | 1843 | Ms. | | 22U | attorney | 12,000 | C | Ca |
| E. Howard McCaleb, Jr.* | 1868 | La. (N.O.) | | 69U | attorney | 5,000 | P | Ca |
| Frank L. McCaleb* | 1876 | La. | | 22U | cashier | | | Ca |
| Bernard McCloskey* | 1860 | Ireland | | 7U | attorney | 12,500 | P | Ca |
| Ivy E. McConnell* | 1869 | La. | | 14U | bookkeeper | | | Ca |

| Name | Birth | Origin | | Code | Occupation | Value | | |
|---|---|---|---|---|---|---|---|---|
| John J. McCormick* | 1873 | La. | yes | 9U | prison commissary contractor | | | Ca |
| John F. McCoy* | 1860 | La. | yes | :5U | | | | |
| William McCue* | 1874 | La. (N.O.) | yes | 22D | bartender | 1,200 | E | Ca |
| William R. McDonald* | | La. | | 4D[30] | machinist[31] | | | Pr |
| Charles P. McEnery* | 1879 | La. | yes | 20U | postmaster[32] | | | |
| Thomas J. McEvoy* | 1865 | La. | yes | 21U | feed merchant | 7,250 | | |
| William C. McGeehan* | 1846 | La. (N.O.) | | 25U | collector | 1,450 | E | Ca |
| John McGuire* | 1854 | La. | | 16D | railroad agent | 4,200 | | |
| Orris I. McLellan* | 1853 | La. (N.O.) | | A | dock company president | 100,250[33] | | |
| Hugh McManus* | 1838 | Ireland | | 12U | homestead director, stave merchant | 26,710 | | Ca |
| Charles A. McMurray† | 1853 | La. (N.O.) | yes | 49U | clerk | | | |
| Henry B. McMurray* | 1856 | La. (N.O.) | yes | 42U | civil sheriff | 7,000 | S | Ca |
| James W. McRacken* | 1858 | La. | | 23D | bookkeeper | 4,950 | B | |
| Thomas L. Macon, Jr.* | 1868 | La. | | 65U | grocer, brewer | | | |
| Charles T. Madison† | 1870 | La. | | 53U | attorney | | P | |
| Thomas F. Maher* | 1857 | La. (N.O.) | yes | A | judge | 2,700 | S | Ca |
| James A. Malloy* | 1856 | La. (N.O.) | yes | 31U | court clerk | 2,200 | E | Ca |
| Robert J. Maloney* | 1871 | La. | yes | 21U | attorney | 2,400 | P | Ca |
| Joseph E. Manning* | 1865 | La. (N.O.) | yes | 17U | paving contractor | | | Ca |
| Sidney March* | 1866 | La. (N.O.) | yes | 17U | banker | 6,000 | | J |
| Frank S. Marks* | 1868 | La. | | 22D | court clerk | | | |
| Andrew P. Marmouget† | 1858 | La. (N.O.) | yes | 66D | judge | 2,200 | | Ca |
| Armand Mary* | 1859 | N.Y. | yes | 17D | dentist | | | |
| Henry Maspero* | 1859 | La. (N.O.) | | 20D | stockbroker | | B | |
| Frank J. Matthew* | 1864 | La. (N.O.) | yes | 39U | house painter | 6,250 | B | |

| NAME | YEAR OF BIRTH | PLACE OF BIRTH | IMMIGRANT PARENT(S) | 1900 RESIDENCE (DISTANCE FROM CITY CORE IN BLOCKS) | 1900 OCCUPATION | 1902 WEALTH | EDUCATION | RELIGION |
|---|---|---|---|---|---|---|---|---|
| Gustav Mauberret* | 1856 | La. (N.O.) | yes | 14D | clerk | 2,500 | C | Ca |
| Leon E. Mauberret* | 1875 | La. (N.O.) | | 14D | government clerk | 2,930 | S | Ca |
| Victor Mauberret* | 1852 | La. (N.O.) | yes | 14D | printer | 1,050[34] | | Ca |
| Edward S. Maunsell† | 1854 | La. (N.O.) | | 32D | insurance agent | | | |
| Daniel A. Mayert | 1850 | La. (N.O.) | yes | 23U | liquor dealer | | | J |
| William Mehle* | 1843 | La. (N.O.) | yes | 24U | hides merchant, councilman | 9,200 | E | Ca |
| Baptiste Melun* | 1871 | La. | yes | 45D | dairy farmer | | | Ca |
| Adolph Meyer* | 1842 | Ms. | yes | 6U | United States Congressman, cotton broker | 15,050 | C | J |
| Victor Meyer* | 1844 | Ms. | yes | 6U | merchant | 2,000 | | J |
| John T. Michel* | 1858 | La. | | 53U | secretary of state | 2,500 | E | Ca |
| Bernard Michell* | 1855 | England | | 28D | river pilot | | E | |
| George A. Middlemiss* | 1873 | La. (N.O.) | yes | 23U | city engineer | | | |
| T. Marshall Miller* | 1847 | Ms. | | 22U | attorney | 8,500[35] | P | Pr |
| William Miller* | 1869 | La. (N.O.) | yes | 34U | sheriff's keeper | | | Ca |
| John G. Mioton, Jr.* | 1868 | La. (N.O.) | | 25D | insurance agent | | C | Ca |
| S. Fitzhugh Mioton* | 1873 | La. | | 24D | physician | | | Ca |
| Peter W. Mohan* | 1875 | La. | | 20U | private collector | 600 | | |
| Frank Adair Monroe* | 1844 | Md. | | 8U | supreme court justice | | C | Pr |
| Henry Mooney* | 1874 | La. (N.O.) | | 60U | attorney | 8,900[36] | P | Pr |
| Isaiah Moore* | 1846 | British West Indies | | 28U | judge | | C | J |

| Name | Year | Place | | Code | Occupation | Value | | |
|---|---|---|---|---|---|---|---|---|
| Thomas J. Moran* | 1845 | La. (N.O.) | yes | 15U | stationer | 15,000 | | Ca |
| Ralph C. Morgan† | 1853 | La. | | 15D | grocery clerk | | | Ca |
| Henry Morvan* | 1874 | La. (N.O.) | yes | 10U | photographer | | | Ca |
| Thomas J. Moulin† | 1856 | La. (N.O.) | yes | 26D | city controller | | | |
| Louis R. Moustier* | 1876 | La. (N.O.) | | 17U | bookkeeper | | | Ca |
| Frank P. Mullen† | 1864 | D.C. | yes | 11U | asphalt contractor | | | Ca |
| Walter C. Murphy† | 1861 | La. (N.O.) | yes | 12U | canal superintendent | | S | Ca |
| William B. Murphy* | 1861 | La. (N.O.) | yes | 23U | court clerk | | | Ca |
| Christopher E. Murray* | 1853 | La. (N.O.) | yes | 49U | judge | 1,650[37] | | Ca |
| John Murray* | 1868 | La. | yes | 21U | deputy sheriff | | | |
| William Murray* | 1843 | England | | 11U | railroad agent, police commissioner | 4,000[38] | | |
| William Nelson† | 1850 | La. (N.O.) | yes | 16U | docking clerk | 800[39] | | |
| Charles Noel† | 1864 | La. (N.O.) | yes | 43D | government clerk | | B | Ca |
| Albert P. Noll* | 1847 | Pa. | yes | 21D | insurance agent | 7,850 | | |
| Charles D. O'Connor* | 1864 | La. (N.O.) | | 9U | laundry owner | 9,500 | E | Ca |
| Frederick O'Donnell* | 1880 | N.Y. | yes | 13U | art printer | | | |
| Peter J. O'Reilly* | 1831 | Ireland | | 2D | elevator maker | 13,000 | | |
| William J. Oberle* | 1857 | La. (N.O.) | yes | 52U | broker | 4,000 | E | Ca |
| Gustave Oertling† | 1867 | La. | | 18D | brewer | 1,600 | | |
| William C. Oertling* | 1851 | La. | yes | 18D | clerk | | | |
| John G. Oriol* | 1860 | La. | | 33D | lumber inspector | | | |
| Fernand Paletou† | 1874 | La. (N.O.) | yes | 9D | clerk | | E | |
| Louis P. Paquet* | 1869 | Tx. | | 47U | attorney | | C | |
| C. Harrison Parker* | 1846 | Pa. | yes | 15U | tax collector | | S | |
| Arthur J. Parody* | 1873 | La. (N.O.) | yes | 25U | railroad clerk | | | |

| NAME | YEAR OF BIRTH | PLACE OF BIRTH | IMMIGRANT PARENT(S) | 1900 RESIDENCE (DISTANCE FROM CITY CORE IN BLOCKS) | 1900 OCCUPATION | 1902 WEALTH | EDUCATION | RELIGION |
|---|---|---|---|---|---|---|---|---|
| Philip J. Patorno* | 1866 | Italy | | 11D | judge | 4,400 | P | |
| Mercer W. Patton* | 1868 | La. | | 27U | attorney | | P | Ca |
| Henry R. Pedarre* | 1860 | La. (N.O.) | | 37D | awning dealer | 2,200[40] | | Ca |
| Richard Peete* | 1870 | La. | | 53U | attorney | | P | |
| James B. Pelletier* | 1857 | La. (N.O.) | yes | 14D | money broker | | | Pr |
| George B. Penrose* | 1857 | La. (N.O.) | | 23U | city treasurer | | C | Ca |
| Henry Peters* | 1849 | La. (N.O.) | yes | 17D | stevedore | 7,500[41] | | Ca |
| Theodore Peters* | 1877 | La. (N.O.) | yes | 18D | attorney | | P | Ca |
| Alfred S. Phelps* | 1864 | La. (N.O.) | | 25U | railroad agent | | | |
| Maurice Picheloup* | 1866 | La. (N.O.) | yes | 42D | dairyman | 4,700 | | Ca |
| George Porteous† | | | | 63U[42] | plant manager[43] | 6,000[44] | | |
| Charles Post† | 1869 | La. (N.O.) | | 62U | river pilot | 2,700 | | |
| George W. Prados* | 1852 | La. (N.O.) | | 29D | court clerk | 1,275 | | |
| Henry Puderer* | 1861 | La. (N.O.) | yes | 47U | government clerk | 2,800 | | Pr |
| Alexander Pujol* | 1860 | La. (N.O.) | yes | 23D | assessor | 3,550 | E | Ca |
| Lamar C. Quintero* | 1863 | Mexico | | 35D | attorney | 3,500[45] | P | Ca |
| Frank E. Rainold* | 1865 | La. | | 64U | attorney | 12,000 | | |
| Henry C. Ramos† | 1856 | In. | yes | 10D | saloon owner | 25,800 | | |
| Martial H. Redon* | 1852 | France | | 2D[46] | bookmaker[47] | | | |
| Terence Reilly* | 1846 | Ireland | | 14U | clerk | 7,500 | | |
| William Reinerth* | 1849 | La. (N.O.) | | 18D | hat dealer | 3,400 | | |
| William H. Reynolds† | 1866 | La. (N.O.) | yes | 37U | iron manufacturer | 10,000[48] | | |
| William Markham Rhodus† | 1861 | La. | | 40U | lumber dealer | 1,350 | | |

| Name | Year | Birthplace | | Age | Occupation | Wealth | | |
| --- | --- | --- | --- | --- | --- | --- | --- | --- |
| Louis Rice* | 1857 | La. (N.O.) | | 39U | saddler | 21,500 | C | Ca |
| Louis A. Richard* | 1848 | La. | yes | 29D | auctioneer | 500[49] | | Ca |
| Mentor V. Richard* | 1850 | La. | | 23U | physician | | P | |
| Clay Riggs* | 1854 | La. | | 7U | cistern maker | 1,600 | P | Ca |
| Edward Rightor* | 1874 | La. | | 43U | attorney | | P | Ca |
| Alonzo Robert† | 1861 | La. | | 49U | accountant | 2,600 | | |
| Joseph L. Rock†* | 1859 | La. (N.O.) | yes | 14D | government clerk | 500[50] | | Pr |
| Wynne Rogers* | 1845 | La. (N.O.) | yes | 12U | attorney, judge | 3,300 | P | Pr |
| Charles J. Russell* | 1871 | La. (N.O.) | | 11U | court clerk | | B | |
| Thomas J. Ryan* | 1853 | La. | yes | 30U | telegraph clerk | 600 | | Ca |
| John St. Paul* | 1867 | Al. | yes | 21D | judge | | P | Ca |
| Anthony Sambola* | 1836 | La. (N.O.) | yes | 27D | attorney | | P | |
| Frank Satimore† | 1858 | N.Y. | yes | 12U | cigar dealer | 5,800[51] | | Ca |
| George A. Scheib* | 1874 | La. (N.O.) | yes | 7U | saloon keeper | 500[52] | | Pr |
| Charles H. Schenck* | 1838 | Germany | | 15U | banker | 35,000 | | |
| Henry B. Schreiber* | 1860 | La. (N.O.) | yes | 35U | grain merchant | 7,200 | | |
| Gabriel A. Scooler* | 1873 | La. (N.O.) | yes | 12U | jeweler | | | |
| William E. Seebold, Jr.* | 1871 | La. | yes | 17U | manufacturer's agent | | | |
| Bernard C. Shields* | 1853 | La. (N.O.) | | 76U | bookkeeper, councilman | 5,500 | P | |
| Abraham Silverstein* | 1876 | La. | yes | 24U | crockery dealer | | | |
| Felix L. Simon* | 1860 | La. (N.O.) | yes | 22D[53] | clerk[54] | | | |
| Mark C. Sintes* | 1857 | Spain | | 29U | contractor | 11,000 | P | |
| Walter B. Sommerville* | 1854 | La. (N.O.) | | 35U | city attorney | 4,500 | P | |
| Charles T. Soniat* | 1847 | La. (N.O.) | yes | 3D | attorney | 6,000 | P | |
| Gustave V. Soniat* | 1856 | La. | | 17U | attorney | 3,000 | P | Ca |
| Jacob Spitzfaden* | 1854 | La. (N.O.) | yes | 15D | real estate | 3,500 | E | Pr |

| NAME | YEAR OF BIRTH | PLACE OF BIRTH | IMMIGRANT PARENT(S) | 1900 RESIDENCE (DISTANCE FROM CITY CORE IN BLOCKS) | 1900 OCCUPATION | 1902 WEALTH | EDUCATION | RELIGION |
|---|---|---|---|---|---|---|---|---|
| Henry F. Stanley* | 1853 | Ireland | | 24U | railroad foreman | | | |
| Clark Steen* | 1855 | La. (N.O.) | yes | 19U | government clerk | | | |
| Val J. Stentz* | 1873 | La. (N.O.) | | 50U | attorney | 400 | P | Ca |
| John M. Stewart† | | | | 21U[55] | agent[56] | | | |
| Peter Stifft† | 1866 | La. | yes | 14U | attorney | 3,800[57] | P | Ca |
| Paul Stoltz* | 1857 | La. (N.O.) | yes | 38U | tax collector | | | Pr |
| Charles B. Stroudback* | 1863 | La. (N.O.) | yes | 41U | insurance agent | | | Ca |
| Charles Sturges* | 1847 | La. (N.O.) | | 35D | collector | | | Ca |
| Bartholomew P. Sullivan* | 1858 | La. (N.O.) | yes | 23U | stationer | 3,450 | S | |
| John P. Sullivan* | 1875 | La. (N.O.) | yes | 42U | attorney | | P | Ca |
| James G. Swarbrickt* | 1869 | La. | yes | 14U | grocer | | | Ca |
| George W. Taylort | 1860 | La. | yes | 29U | merchant | 8,500 | | |
| Joseph Dewey Taylor† | 1842 | In. | | 9U | notary | 50 | S | Pr |
| Christopher H. Tebault* | 1840 | Ms. | | 5U | physician | | P | Ca |
| J. R. Terhune* | | | | 18U[58] | telegraph manager[59] | | | |
| Alfred F. Theard* | 1865 | La. (N.O.) | | 26D | government engineer | | C | Ca |
| George H. Theard* | 1857 | La. (N.O.) | | 10D | judge | | P | Ca |
| Thomas Thiel† | 1865 | La. | | 7D | bartender | | | |
| Frank B. Thomas* | 1863 | La. (N.O.) | | 35U | attorney | | S | |
| Frank P. Thriffely* | 1850 | La. | yes | 23D | grocer | 17,150 | | |
| John F. Tims* | 1859 | La. (N.O.) | | 47U | government clerk | | E | Ca |

| Name | Year | Origin | | Code | Occupation | Value ($) | | |
|---|---|---|---|---|---|---|---|---|
| John R. Todd* | 1842 | La. (N.O.) | | 16U | jury commissioner | | E | Pr |
| Willard Todd* | 1861 | Ia. | | 27U | civil engineer | | P | |
| Carsten E. Torjuson* | 1859 | Norway | | 19U | captain, attorney | 12,600 | | |
| Joseph Tranchina†* | 1853 | Italy | | 16U | contractor | 8,100 | | |
| George A. Trauth* | 1851 | Germany | | 79U | saloon keeper | | C | Pr |
| Orense A. Trezevant† | 1868 | Scotland | yes | 7D | assessor | 2,800[60] | S | Ca |
| Vital Tujague* | 1872 | La. (N.O.) | | 29D | city comptroller | | | |
| Thomas J. Tully, Jr.* | 1856 | La. | | 44U | travel agent[61] | | S | |
| William G. Turner* | 1866 | Ws. | yes | A | cotton press owner | | | |
| Henry N. Umbach* | 1851 | La. | yes | 13U | tax collector | 2,000[62] | S | Pr |
| George W. Vandervort† | 1868 | Ms. | yes | 41U | police secretary | | | Pr |
| Henry A. Veters* | | La. (N.O.) | | 3U | hat merchant | 400 | | |
| J. J. Waddill* | | | | | fertilizer inspector | | | |
| Benjamin T. Waldo† | 1872 | La. (N.O.) | | 60U | attorney | | P | Ca |
| Blayney T. Walshe†* | 1840 | Ireland | yes | 55U | tax collector | 2,800[63] | | Pr |
| George C. Walshe† | 1866 | La. (N.O.) | | 51U | attorney | 4,000 | P | Pr |
| William J. Warren* | 1858 | England | | 30D | civil engineer | | | |
| Edward S. Whitaker* | 1854 | S.C. | | 11U | attorney | | | |
| Edmond P. White* | 1862 | Mo. | | 45U | contractor | 8,000 | E | Ca |
| Fernand J. White* | 1862 | La. (N.O.) | yes | 30D | court clerk | | E | |
| William H. Wilkinson | 1854 | La. | | 10U | bartender | | | |
| Julius D. Willis†* | 1857 | Ms. | | 44U | contractor | | | Pr |
| Lawrence C. Wilt* | 1855 | La. | yes | 14D | cafe owner | 7,000 | | |
| Richard Davezac Winship† | | | | 22U[64] | broker[65] | | | |
| Charles Wirth* | 1851 | Germany | | 36U | grocer | 66,800 | P | Pr |
| Isadore S. Wolff† | 1859 | La. (N.O.) | | 10D | laborer | 3,500 | | |
| John A. Woodville* | 1874 | Honduras | | 24U | attorney | | | |

| NAME | YEAR OF BIRTH | PLACE OF BIRTH | IMMIGRANT PARENT(S) | 1900 RESIDENCE (DISTANCE FROM CITY CORE IN BLOCKS) | 1900 OCCUPATION | 1902 WEALTH | EDUCATION | RELIGION |
|---|---|---|---|---|---|---|---|---|
| Wilson M. Wren* | 1872 | La. | | 43U | streetcar conductor | 150 | | |
| Charles T. Yenni* | 1860 | La. (N.O.) | | 83U | photographer | | E | |
| C. P. Young* | | | | 70U[66] | accountant[67] | | | |
| James S. Zacherie* | 1844 | La. (N.O.) | yes | 26U | real estate, councilman | 3,800 | C | Pr |
| Henry L. Zander* | 1860 | La. (N.O.) | yes | 12D | government draughtsman | 1,900 | P | |
| Frank Zengal* | 1866 | La. (N.O.) | yes | 24D | attorney | | P | Ca |
| Frederick Zengal* | 1855 | La. (N.O.) | yes | 25D | city notary | 5,900 | E | Ca |

APPENDIX NOTES:

1. 1900 wealth.
2. 1900 wealth.
3. 1900 wealth.
4. 1900 wealth.
5. 1900 wealth.
6. 1900 wealth.
7. 1897 occupation.
8. 1898 occupation.
9. 1900 wealth.
10. 1900 wealth.
11. 1902 residence.
12. 1902 occupation.
13. 1901 residence.
14. 1901 occupation.
15. 1909 occupation.
16. 1900 wealth.
17. 1900 wealth.
18. 1900 wealth.
19. 1901 wealth.
20. 1900 wealth.
21. 1902 occupation.
22. 1898 occupation.
23. 1900 wealth.
24. 1897 residence.
25. 1897 occupation.
26. 1900 wealth.
27. 1902 occupation.
28. 1900 wealth.
29. 1900 wealth.
30. 1903 residence.
31. 1903 occupation.
32. 1902 occupation.
33. 1900 wealth.
34. 1900 wealth.
35. 1900 wealth.
36. 1900 wealth.

| | |
|---|---|
| 37. | 1900 wealth. |
| 38. | 1900 wealth. |
| 39. | 1900 wealth. |
| 40. | 1900 wealth. |
| 41. | 1900 wealth. |
| 42. | 1897 residence. |
| 43. | 1898 occupation. |
| 44. | 1900 wealth. |
| 45. | 1900 wealth. |
| 46. | 1903 residence. |
| 47. | 1908 occupation. |

| | |
|---|---|
| 48. | 1900 wealth. |
| 49. | 1900 wealth. |
| 50. | 1900 wealth. |
| 51. | 1900 wealth. |
| 52. | 1900 wealth. |
| 53. | 1898 residence. |
| 54. | 1898 occupation. |
| 55. | 1898 residence. |
| 56. | 1898 occupation. |
| 57. | 1900 wealth. |

| | |
|---|---|
| 58. | 1902 residence. |
| 59. | 1902 occupation. |
| 60. | 1900 wealth. |
| 61. | 1901 occupation. |
| 62. | 1900 wealth. |
| 63. | 1900 wealth. |
| 64. | 1898 residence. |
| 65. | 1898 occupation. |
| 66. | 1907 residence. |
| 67. | 1907 occupation. |

KEY: In the listings above, the cross (†) indicates that the person was a charter member of the Choctaw Club of Louisiana. The asterisk (*) indicates that the person was a member of the Choctaw Club in 1902. The abbreviations have the following meanings: U-Uptown above Canal Street; D-Downtown below Canal Street; A-Algiers; E-Elementary education; S-Secondary education; B-Business school; C-College education; P-Professional and/or graduate education; Ca-Catholic; Pr-Protestant; J-Jewish.

SOURCES: Manuscript Census Returns, Tenth Census of the United States, 1880; Twelfth Census of the United States, 1900; Thirteenth Census of the United States, 1910; Louisiana, Orleans Parish, Records of the United States Bureau of the Census; City of New Orleans Real Estate Tax Ledgers, 1896-1897, 1900-1902; *Soards' New Orleans City Directory,* 1896-1910; *Tulane News Bulletin,* 1921-1930; *The Citizens' League: A History of the Great Reform Movement in New Orleans, April 21, 1896* (New Orleans, n. d.); "Choctaw Club of Louisiana," *Club Life,* Special Edition (May 1902); New Orleans press, especially *Daily Picayune,* 1896-1914; *Times-Democrat,* 1896-1914; *Times-Picayune,* 1914-1954; *Daily States,* 1896-1954; *Item,* 1896-1954; and various other primary and secondary sources, published and unpublished.

# Essay on Sources

Prosopographic studies such as this one employ a wide variety of primary and secondary sources. The most important primary source for this work was the Twelfth United States Census of Population, 1900, Louisiana, Volumes 24-31, Orleans Parish, New Orleans City. The manuscript census records provided information on the birthplaces, ages, nationalities of parents, occupations and years of residence in the United States of the members of the Citizens' League of New Orleans and the Choctaw Club of Louisiana, respectively. Those New Orleans political leaders who did not appear in the 1900 census were often present in the Tenth United States Census of Population, 1880, Louisiana, and the Twelfth United States Census of Population, 1910, Louisiana.

New Orleans newspapers also provided a wealth of information on the Crescent City politicos. The press commonly carried biographical sketches of candidates during election campaigns and often ran stories on particular professions such as the members of the New Orleans bar. Obituaries, however, constituted the most useful source for details on religion, education, family ties, occupational associations and organizational memberships. Of particular help were the Obituary Files, Louisiana Division, New Orleans Public Library. These records greatly facilitated the use of the New Orleans *Daily Picayune*, New Orleans *Daily States*, New Orleans *Times-Democrat*, New Orleans *Item* and New Orleans *Times-Picayune*.

Biographical sketches of New Orleans politicians also appeared in *The Citizens' League: A History of the Great Reform Movement in New Orleans, April 21, 1896* (New Orleans, n.

d.); "The Choctaw Club of Louisiana," *Club Life*, Special Edition (May 1902); and Democratic Party, Louisiana Central Committee, *The Convention of '98: A Complete Work on the Greatest Event in Louisiana's History, Together with a Historical Review of the Conventions of the Past and the General Assembly Which Called the Constitutional Convention* (New Orleans, 1898). Several publications featured biographical profiles of prominent Louisianians. Among these works were *Who's Who in Louisiana and Mississippi* (New Orleans, 1918); *Biographical and Historical Memoirs of Louisiana*, 2 vols. (Chicago, 1892); John Smith Kendall, *History of New Orleans*, 3 vols. (Chicago, 1922); Alcée Fortier, *Louisiana*, 3 vols. (Madison, Wisconsin, 1914); and *The Israelites of Louisiana* (New Orleans, n. d.). They, like the newspaper sketches, were useful for information on religion, education, family ties, occupational associations and social connections.

City directories also supplied valuable information on the addresses, business associations and occupations of Crescent City politicos. Individuals who did not show up in any other source were often included in the city directories. Because these volumes usually listed the home addresses of the politicians, they were essential to the use of the manuscript census records. The city directories also enumerated the various governmental offices held by the political leaders. So, too, did *Municipal Manual of the City of New Orleans, 1903* (New Orleans, 1903); Louisiana Legislative Council, *Membership in the Legislature of Louisiana, 1880-1980* (Baton Rouge, 1979); and Official Roll of General Assembly of the State of Louisiana, 1900, Louisiana Collection, Howard-Tilton Memorial Library, Tulane University, New Orleans, Louisiana.

Several items contained information on the previous political involvement of New Orleans reformers. These included the Justin F. Denechaud Papers, Louisiana Historical Center, Louisiana State Museum, Old U. S. Mint Building, New Orleans, Louisiana; Berthold C. Alwes, "The History of the Louisiana State Lottery Company, *Louisiana*

*Historical Quarterly,"* XXVII (October 1927); and *Official Report of the Proceedings of the Anti-Lottery Democratic Convention Held in the Hall of the House of Representatives, Baton Rouge, La. on Thursday and Friday, August 7 and 8, 1890* (New Orleans, 1890). Denechaud was a leader in the Anti-Lottery League whose papers contained the minutes of several reform meetings that included the names of those members who were in attendance. On April 2, 1896, the New Orleans *Daily Picayune* published a list of all candidates for municipal office since 1878 with their political affiliations.

The only available source on the wealth of Crescent City political leaders was the City of New Orleans Real Estate Tax Ledgers, 1896-1902, City Archives, Louisiana Division, New Orleans Public Library. These documents required painstaking analysis and accounted solely for real estate holdings. Other types of property and monetary wealth went unrecorded.

Several issues of the *Tulane News Bulletin* were useful for information on politicians, specially doctors and lawyers, who attended that university. The publication frequently listed the members of graduating classes, courses of study, hometowns, birthdates and deathdates. Several sources, primary and secondary, listed the social affiliations of New Orleans politicians. These included *Membership Roster of New Orleans Clubs, 1899* (New Orleans, 1899); *Combined Rosters of City Lodges, F. and A. M.* (New Orleans, 1914); *Souvenir Program: Elks Burlesque Circus* (New Orleans, 1906); *New Orleans Chess, Checkers and Whist Club* (New Orleans, 1912 and 1913); Stuart O. Landry, *History of the Boston Club* (New Orleans, 1938); and Augusto P. Miceli, *The Pickwick Club of New Orleans* (New Orleans, 1964).

Secondary sources provided worthwhile background information on the Crescent City. John Smith Kendall, *History of New Orleans*, 3 vols. (Chicago, 1922); Joe Gary Taylor, *Louisiana Reconstructed, 1863-1877* (Baton Rouge, 1974); and Walter Prichard, ed., "The Origin and Activities of the 'White League' in New Orleans (Reminiscences of a Participant in the Movement)," *Louisiana Historical Quarterly*, XXIII (April 1940), are important sources for the development of New Orleans politics during Reconstruction. Joe Gray Taylor, *Louisiana: A Bicentennial History* (New York, 1976); William Ivy Hair, *Bourbonism and Agrarian Protest: Louisiana Politics, 1877-1900* (Baton Rouge, 1969); and Charles L. Dufour, *Ten Flags in the Wind: The Story of Louisiana* (New York, 1967), are state studies with useful information on the Crescent City.

The best modern treatment of New Orleans politics in the late nineteenth century is Joy Jackson, *New Orleans in the Gilded Age: Politics and Urban Progress, 1880-1896* (Baton Rouge, 1969). Wayne M. Everard, "Bourbon City: New Orleans, 1878-1900," *Louisiana Studies*, XI (Fall 1972), covers the same topic from the perspective of New South history. Brian Gary Ettinger, "John Fitzpatrick and the Limits of Working-Class Politics in New Orleans, 1892-1896," *Louisiana History*, XXVI (Fall 1985), is a worthwhile study. Raymond O. Nussbaum, "'The Ring Is Smashed!': The New Orleans Municipal Election of 1896," *Louisiana History*, XVII (Summer 1976), carefully examines the forces that contributed to the victory of the Citizens' League. His "Progressive Politics in New Orleans, 1896-1900," (Ph.D. dissertation, Tulane University, 1974), is a valuable study of the reform organization in power and its ultimate demise. Matthew J. Schott, "John M. Parker of Louisiana and the Varieties of American Progressivism" (Ph.D. dissertation, Vanderbilt University, 1969), is a fine work that focuses on the most successful New Orleans reformer.

Hair, *Bourbonism and Agrarian Protest*; J. Morgan Kousser, *The Shaping of Southern Politics: Suffrage Restriction and the Establishment of the One-Party South, 1880-1910* (New Haven, 1974); and Matthew J. Schott, "Progressives Against Democracy: Electoral Reform in Louisiana, 1894-1921," *Louisiana History*, XX (Summer 1979), examine the disfranchisement convention of 1898 from different perspectives. George E. Cunningham, "The Italian, a Hinderance to White Solidarity in Louisiana," *Journal of Negro History*, L (January 1965), focuses on the question of immigrant voting. William Ivy Hair, *Carnival of Fury: Robert Charles and the New Orleans Race Riot of 1900* (Baton Rouge, 1976); David C. Rankin, "The Impact of the Civil War on the Free Colored Community of New Orleans," *Perspectives in American History*, XI (1977-1978); and Dale A. Somers, "Black and White in New Orleans: A Study in Urban Race Relations, 1865-1900," *Journal of Southern History*, XL (February 1974), discuss racial conditions in the Crescent City during the late nineteenth century. Henry C. Dethloff, "Populism and Reform in Louisiana," (Ph.D. dissertation, University of Missouri, 1964), covers the racial views of New Orleans reformers.

There is no study of New Orleans politics in the early twentieth century that is comparable to the Jackson work, but George M. Reynolds, *Machine Politics in New Orleans, 1897-1926* (New York, 1936); and Harold Zink, *City Bosses in the United States: A Study of Twenty Municipal Bosses* (Durham, N. C., 1930), are older works that remain useful. Both contain valuable biographical sketches of Martin Behrman. Also significant is John R. Kemp, ed., *Martin Behrman of New Orleans: Memoirs of a City Boss* (Baton Rouge, 1977), a condensed version of Behrman's memoirs that appeared in the New Orleans *Item* in 1922. Kemp's introduction is an important modern supplement to the Zink and Reynolds volumes. T. Harry Williams, *Huey Long* (New York, 1969); and Allan P. Sindler, *Huey Long's Louisiana: State Politics, 1920-1952* (Baltimore, 1956), are works on the Louisiana Kingfish that also discuss the power of the New Orleans machine in state politics.

Federal Writers' Project, *The WPA Guide to New Orleans* (Boston, 1938); Pierce F. Lewis, *New Orleans: The Making of an Urban Landscape* (Cambridge, 1976); Hair, *Carnival of Fury*; and Wilton P. Ledet, "The History of the City of Carrollton," *Louisiana Historical Quarterly*, XXI (January 1938), are useful for the study of urban expansion in New Orleans. Raymond A. Mohl, *The New City: Urban America in the In-*

*dustrial Age, 1860-1920* (Arlington Heights, 1985); David R. Goldfield and Blaine A. Brownell, *Urban America: From Downtown to No Town* (Boston, 1979); Howard P. Chudacoff, *The Evolution of American Urban Society* (Englewood Cliffs, 1981 edition); and Alexander B. Callow, Jr., *The City Boss in America* (New York, 1976), are modern studies of political conflict in urban America that note political trends in New Orleans. Samuel P. Hays, "The Politics of Reform in Municipal Government in the Progressive Era," *Pacific Northwest Quarterly*, LV (October 1964), is a classic examination of urban reformers. William L. Riordon, *Plunkitt of Tammany Hall* (New York, 1948, 1963), presents the viewpoints of New York machine boss George Washington Plunkitt whose political opinions were remarkably similar to several of the thoughts that Martin Behrman advanced in his published memoirs.

# INDEX